MILTON'S ROYALISM

MILTON'S ROYALISM

A Study of the Conflict of Symbol
and Idea in the Poems

BY

MALCOLM MACKENZIE ROSS

NEW YORK / RUSSELL & RUSSELL

CORNELL STUDIES IN ENGLISH

VOLUME XXXIV

TO MY MOTHER

Preface

THIS study attempts to analyze and to explain the use of royalist symbolism in the anti-royalist context of John Milton's poetry. I see Milton as a poet caught in a period of abrupt revolutionary change, a period in which fundamental values were shifting and dissolving. When the head of Charles I dropped into the basket, the literary artist was deprived of a whole world of symbolism. For a century of writers the crown, "the imperial theme," had been an emotive staple, a bright and sensuous metaphor by which political, moral, and aesthetic virtues could be suggested. Prince Hal is transformed by the magic of the crown. Spenser's moral theme is expressed in strictly royalist terms. John Donne's Court of Heaven is in the image of the Court of England.

With the ripening of open class hostility into Civil War, "the crown" could no longer symbolize all-inclusive social and personal values. The connotation of royalism had changed—even for its supporters. Yet Milton, writing as a bitter anti-royalist, drew heavily on the royalist literary tradition. A contradiction between the symbol and the idea was inevitable. There is evidence that Milton became aware of this contradiction in *Paradise Lost,* and sought in the last poems to purify his idiom.

In order to understand fully the dilemma in which Milton found himself it is necessary to recognize the significance for Elizabethan literature of a correspondence, however precarious, between aesthetic and social values. Milton in his use of political and social symbols comes at the end of a great tradition. Obviously the Puritan rejection of the monarchy as a guarantee and symbol of order, and the Puritan acceptance of social division and strife as the predestined prelude to the enjoyment of a free Christian society, must involve for literature a qualitative change in values. Neither the national theme nor the religious theme could have the same implication for Milton as it had for the patriotic Elizabethan. The God who sanctioned the execution of Charles I could not be represented in quite the same way as the God who "saved" Good Queen Bess. And yet the ultimate disintegration of royalist symbolism evident in Milton's poetry is inherent in Elizabethanism itself, more specifically in the perishable nature of the "class compromise" which underlined Elizabethan culture for a few brief glorious years. If Milton reaps the fine harvest of Elizabethan poetry—he reaps the whirlwind, too. He is the victim of what the sociologists call "the cultural lag"—the persistence of literary and aesthetic values in a social milieu which now contradicted them. The origins of this contradiction, the origins of the aesthetic problem which confronted Milton, go back to the Elizabethan age itself. My first chapter, then, is inevitably concerned with origins.

The approach to Milton here is of necessity "sociological." I am dealing with the point of shock, the actual impact of social forces on the kind and quality of Milton's political symbolism. It is my hope that such a study will not only throw new light on the aesthetic and technical problems which confronted Milton, but that it will also contribute something to the general knowledge of the relation of art to society.

I have aimed not so much at the presentation of new facts as at a fresh examination of the poetic text and, where necessary, at a reinterpretation and digestion of already available material. The reader is asked to bear in mind that my treatment of Milton in this book is a *conscious* over-simplification.

PREFACE

I have not thought it necessary or desirable to review at all points the maze of literary and personal influences which unquestionably helped to shape the direction of Milton's work. It is my belief that the student of Milton can readily adapt my findings to a broader perspective.

My debts are many. I have, of course, drawn heavily and gratefully on the work of Professor James Holly Hanford, Sir Herbert Grierson, and Dr. E. M. W. Tillyard. I am deeply indebted to Professor Elkin Wilson's *England's Eliza* for important background material. Professor R. C. Bald has not only given me warm encouragement and critical advice, but has helped me immeasurably in preparing the MS for publication. Professors Herbert Davis, George H. Sabine, William Sale Jr., and G. Wilson Knight have contributed valuable suggestions and criticism. My wife, Lois Ross, took complete charge of the proof-reading and indexing, and aided me in my research. To Professor A. S. P. Woodhouse, for his published work, for his lectures on Milton at the University of Toronto, and for his kind and patient interest in my efforts, I owe a debt which I can never acknowledge sufficiently.

M. M. R.

Key to Abbreviations

OF WORKS FREQUENTLY CITED

Donne:—*Donne's Sermons, Selected Passages,* ed. Logan Pearsall Smith, Oxford, 1920.

Hanford:—J. H. Hanford, *A Milton Handbook,* New York, 1938. This work is sometimes referred to simply as *Handbook.*

Knight:—G. Wilson Knight, *The Imperial Theme,* London, 1931.

L. C. Knights:—L. C. Knights, *Drama and Society in the Age of Jonson,* London, 1937.

Mutchmann:—H. Mutchmann, *Further Studies Concerning the Origin of "Paradise Lost,"* Tartu, 1936.

Of Ref.:—*Of Reformation Touching Church Discipline in England.*

P.L.:—*Paradise Lost.*

P.W.:—*The Prose Works of John Milton,* ed. J. A. St. John (Bohn Library), London, 1848–53.

S.M.:—*The Student's Milton,* ed. Frank Allen Patterson, New York, 1930.

Tillyard:—E. M. W. Tillyard, *Milton,* London, 1930.

U. of T. Quarterly: The University of Toronto Quarterly.

Williams:—Arnold Williams, "Some Conservative Critics of Milton," *Sewanee Review,* XLIV (1941), 90–107.

Wilson:—Elkin Calhoun Wilson, *England's Eliza,* Cambridge, Mass., 1939.

Wright:—Louis B. Wright, *Middle-Class Culture in Elizabethan England,* Chapel Hill, 1935.

Contents

I

The Elizabethan Background

MR. L. C. KNIGHTS, in his admirable book *Drama and Society in the Age of Jonson,* notes a certain unity in Elizabethan culture which seems to defy crude attempts to analyze the literature of the period in terms of class division:

Education, religion, and pastimes, we are told, can all be related to the "prevailing mode of economic production and change"; but that, at present, is an article of faith. And the Marxist diagnosis (with the implication, here, that cultural attributes were *useful* to the leisured class) seems curiously irrevelant when we realize that the interests which I have noted permeated the whole of society; the rhetoric of Shakespeare or Chapman is paralleled at a lower level by the rhetoric of Kyd; the crude psychology of the upper-class "Character" is surpassed by the shrewd folk observation that was to find its supreme expression in Bunyan; and if the plays of Chapman or Tourneur gratified a highly developed taste for moral casuistry, the pamphlets of Dekker indicate that his popular audience had at least some healthy interest in unvarnished morals. Above all there was no barrier of language between higher and lower such as separates the different ranges of the contemporary reading public. The achievement of the great age of English drama (the twenty or twenty-five years, say, from *Troilus and Cressida* and *Henry IV*) was due to the bringing together and fairly lively interplay of different interests within a fairly homogeneous culture at a time "when the art of the people was as closely mingled with the art of the coteries as was the speech of the people that delighted in rhythmical animation, in idiom, in images . . . with the unchanging speech of the poets." *Elizabethan drama, even in its highest ranges, was not the expression of a "class" culture at all.*[1]

[1] L. C. Knights, pp. 10–11; italics mine.

1

This paragraph is a clear-cut, honestly stated challenge to the "sociological" critic of letters—and Mr. Knights is himself a "sociological" critic, and a good one. But to state flatly that Elizabethan drama was "not the expression of a 'class' at all" is only to mislead. The statement misleads all the more because it is superficially true.

Obviously Elizabethan literature is not the product of a single class; nor was it made "to serve the interests" of a single class. It is the product of a "fairly homogeneous" society. For a brief period a cultural synthesis was achieved. To some extent the aims and ideals and methods of the court writers were imitated, or at least paralleled, in the work of the citizens. However, I think it can be shown that two separate traditions did exist without losing their identity, and that, after a period of harmony in which Elizabethan culture seemed unified, the cleavage between Court and City on the economic and political level was reflected on the literary and cultural level. The "fairly homogeneous" society of the great years soon became the sharply divided society of the Caroline period. Instead of saying that the Elizabethan drama, at its highest point, was "not the expression of a 'class' culture at all," Mr. Knights should have said that it was the expression not of a single "class" outlook but of a temporary balance of rival class outlooks.

I fully realize that such a formulation, at first glance, seems mechanical. But when I speak of a "class" literature I do not wish to imply the existence in neat successive compartments of a "feudal" literature, a "bourgeois" literature, and a "semi-feudal" court literature, each with its own appropriate form and technique. Any literary history will demonstrate clearly enough the debt which, in varying degrees, all Elizabethan writers from "the rakehelly rout" to Ben Jonson owe to the classics, to France and Italy, to the native mediaeval tradition, to the language of the Court, to the language of the London streets. Tradition, accident, or the ideal "super-structure" of a society may preponderate in determining the *form* of literature as well as the *form* of historical struggle. It is not my purpose to trace the influence of the woollen industry on English blank verse! The "class" implications of a literature or of a work of art must be investigated and interpreted in terms of the *uncommon denominator,* of the peculiar psychological attitude or bias arising from the economic status or aspiration of the given class. Despite certain similarities of vocabulary, technical devices, etc., sharp and decisive differences between the work of, say, Maxwell Anderson and the earlier Clifford Odets can be easily discovered, differences which are more than differences in personal ability and temperament. One writer wants to conserve society as it is; the other seeks a change, to be brought about by a revolutionary working class. Whether or not Odets was attracted to the working class because of glandular disturbances is of no importance. That a class exists, conscious of its own aims and its own strength, *is* important. The sense of its difference from the possessing class gives rise to a new psychology and a new set of values, which affect deeply the artist who attaches himself to the revolutionary movement.

It has been objected that such a view of the artist as a member of a "class" excludes any understanding of the artist as "a man." One answer to this might be: "To know a man, you must know what is in his head and how it got there!" Or it might be said:

Each man has, as it were, a dual history, since he is at the same time a type, a man with a social history, and an individual, a man with a personal history. The two, of course, even though they may be in glaring conflict, are also one, a unity, in so far as the latter is eventually conditioned by the former, though this does not and should not imply that in art the social type must dominate the individual personality. Falstaff, Don Quixote, Tom Jones, Julien Sorel, Monsieur de Charlus, are all types, but they are types in whom the social characteristics constantly reveal the individual, and in whom the personal hopes, hungers, loves, jealousies and ambitions in turn light up the social background.[2]

The mechanical critic, surely, is the man who isolates the individual from the context of reality. One does not slight the individuality of Shakespeare or Milton by seeking to know, as precisely as possible, those forces which evoked their faith or summoned their despair.

In describing the "class" nature of Elizabethan literature, I wish to show, as clearly as possible, the effect of social and economic transformation on the quality and kind and purpose of the literary work produced. I wish to show that the economic impulses which created an alliance between the aristocracy and the middle class under the benign shadow of the crown, created a *qualitative* set of values, different in kind from the harsh economic and social factors which had generated them, yet that they are dependent upon those factors.

The anarchistic individualism of the market, the dazzling prospect of boundless new worlds to conquer, the real evidence of wealth and power that was now visible in a hitherto provincial London, all served to fire the imagination of poets and playwrights. Perhaps the full-blown quality of artistic individualism in the period is best illustrated in the work of Christopher Marlowe. *Tamburlaine* epitomizes the new and frenzied desire "to take possession of the other seven quadrants," just as Faustus epitomizes the aspiration of the Renaissance mind that would have all knowledge for its province,

[2] Ralph Fox, *The Novel and the People*, p. 25.

and the *Jew of Malta* epitomizes the insatiable, usurious itch for wealth that characterized a generation of conquerors, iconoclasts and monopolists.

In somewhat less spectacular ways the cult of artistic in-dividualism affected the young noblemen who distributed fair copies of their verse to the intimate court circle. Individual self-expression became the fad of the day and, indeed, prefer-ment at court was by no means dissociated from successful verse-making. The anonymous poem was rare enough in this brave new world of courtly "pushers." The search for new forms, verbal surprises, exciting and different suggestions, led the Elizabethan poet away from the mediaeval tradition which he had already discarded in spirit to the poetry of Italy and France and to the Latin and Greek classics.

In saying this I am conscious of saying nothing new. In a vague and broad sense this conventional description of the Renaissance as a burst of individualism in the face of exhilarat-ing forces of change is perfectly true. Individualism stimu-lated the entire age and all classes of society. Too often, perhaps, the phenomenon is attributed to the arrival from Constantinople of refugee scholars clutching the ancient world to their bosoms. Too often the causes are seen in purely literary terms, and I would emphasize the significance of an economic and geographical revolution for the creation of the new spirit. This emphasis too has been made before. Unfortunately, the tendency has been to stop with this emphasis, to admit, in a general sense, the relation of the new birth in culture to the discovery of new worlds to conquer, and to admit no more.

What, then, in the sharpest terms, is the importance for art of this new economic order with its ruthless individualism and its dynamic expansiveness? It adds nothing to our basic under-standing of the period to say that artistic individualism inevitably followed economic individualism. Nor would it be enlightening or even true to make a vast generalization to the effect that Elizabethan literature is the expression of the "revolutionary bourgeoisie." We can, I think, take the obvious for granted and agree that Elizabethan literature owes its freshness, its excitement, its mixed and sometimes awkward splendor, and above all its originality, its genuinely inventive quality, to the great and daring changes abroad in the world. How much further than this can the "sociological approach" go without falling into error of over-simplification?

The most conservative of critics have recognized a "middle-class" Elizabethan literature, just as they have recognized a Court literature, and a literature which transcends (and therefore includes) both.[3] It is not my intention to review at length the work which falls roughly into these separate classifications. But it will be necessary to isolate those values which proceed from and, in their turn, support the class alliance of the period. The importance of cultural unity cannot be fully understood without a clear recognition of the antagonisms which beset it from the beginning, and which finally destroyed it.

L. C. Knights' statement, quoted above, that Elizabethan literature is classless because "the rhetoric of Shakespeare is paralleled at a lower level by the rhetoric of Kyd" is true enough with respect to form and, in a general sense, with respect to the main types of subject matter adopted by writers at both class levels, but it fails to take into account the fierce pride of the citizen in his own class, or the mingled condescension and contempt with which the aristocrat regarded the "new man"—his business associate but scarcely his social

[3] I use the term "class literature" in the psychological sense which I have already described.

equal. "Class consciousness," as we understand the term to-day, was clearly evident in Elizabethan life and letters. Although Court writers heaped ridicule and abuse on the acquisitiveness and lack of gentility displayed by the citizen (a tendency which grew more pronounced in the reign of James and of his son), the bourgeoisie was never silent or docile in the face of this scorn:

But since humility was not a prominent quality in the bourgeois temperament, the citizen did not submit blandly to attacks, and instead of being ashamed of his connection with trade, as might have been the case with a later social-climbing member of the middle class, he set out to prove that he was as good as anybody and to show also that the ideals he stood for were the backbone of the commonwealth. There appeared, therefore, throughout the later sixteenth and first half of the seventeenth centuries a *considerable literature which had for its aim the expression of the middle-class satisfaction in its own position and good qualities. Furthermore, much of this literature was intended to instill a class pride into the minds of the apprentices who would soon occupy positions of importance in the world of trade.*[4]

This pride in class was felt by the stout yeoman as much as by the "middle sort" of the City. When King Edward offers to knight George a Greene, George protests:

I beseech your Grace, grant me one thing.

EDWARD

What is that?

GEORGE

Then let me liue and die a yeoman still.
So was my father, so must liue his sonne.
For tis more credite to men of base degree
To do great deeds, than men of dignitie.[5]

---

[4] Louis B. Wright, *Middle-Class Culture in Elizabethan England*, p. 21; italics mine. The material in this book is extremely useful.

[5] *George a Greene, the Pinner of Wakefield*, lines 1300–1304.

Throughout this play the author—and no doubt the audience, too—take great delight in the easy familiarity between king and yeoman. Edward travels in disguise and rubs shoulders with his subjects as a companionable equal. There is a direct relation between king and people here that needs no noble intermediary or intercessor. George a Greene will accept no courtly title. He chooses to do mighty deeds for the glory of his own class, a class fit to walk with kings, to defend, to advise, and even to instruct the royal person. In the closing lines of the play, when the thwarted James of Scotland requests Edward to fix his ransom, Edward turns to George a Greene:

> George a Greene, set downe the King of Scots
> His ransome.
>
> GEORGE
>
> I beseech your Grace pardon me;
> It passeth my skill.
>
> EDWARD
>
> Do it; the honor's thine.
>
> GEORGE
>
> Then let King James make good
> Those towns which he hath burnt vpon the borders;
> Giue a small pension to the fatherlesse,
> Whose fathers he caus'd murthered in those warres;
> Put in pledge for these things to your grace;
> And so returne.[6]

The king's confidence in George's wisdom is even greater than George's own, but when put to it he asks a ransom not for the greater gain of the king, but for the comfort of the yeomen, the little men who suffered in the wars of kings. And Edward approves, freely and gladly. The king is a friend and honored leader. The yeoman is a counsellor whose merits

[6] *George a Greene,* lines 1306–1316.

are recognized by the king. The dashing courtier is not even shown.

A whole crop of ballads, plays and novels were written to warm the pride of the London apprentice. Many of these, significantly enough, deal with the tried and true friendship of king and citizen:

> And when King Henry stoode in neede
>   of trusty souldiers at command,
> Those prentices prou'de men indeed,
>   and feared no force of warlike band.
> For at the siedge of Tours in France
>   they showed themselues braue English men;
> At Bullein also did aduance
>   S. Georges glorious standard then.
> Let Turwen, Turney, and those townes
>   that good King Henry nobly wonne,
> Tell London prentices renownes,
>   and all the deedes by them there donne.[7]

Another ballad in the Collier collection, revealing this pride of the citizen in the direct company of the king, is entitled: "A delightful song of the four famous feasts of England, the one of them ordained by King Henry the seuenth, to the honour of Merchant Taylors, shewing how seuen Kings haue beene free of that Company, and now lastly graced with the loue of our renowned Prince Henry of Great Britaine."[8]

Perhaps Nicholas Breton has summed up more neatly than any other Elizabethan the citizen's opinion of himself:

Shall the Merchant bee grudged his price of his Wares? what shall I say? who upholds the state of a Citie? or the Honour of a State vnder the King but the Merchant? who beautifieth a Court

---

[7] Reprinted by J. P. Collier (ed.), *Broadside Blackletter Ballads* (London, 1868), pp. 96 ff. Quoted by Wright, p. 28.

[8] Wright, p. 28.

with Jewels and outward ornaments? but the trauell of a Merchant? . . . consider of the sweet ciuill manner of their liues:
whose Houses more neate? whose wiues more modest? whose ap-
parel more comely, whose diet more dainty? and whose carriage
more commendable? valiant without quarrels, merie without mad-
nesse, bountifull in their gifts, . . . and how many poore do they
relieue at home? what Colledges? what Hospitals? what alms-
houses haue they builded? and in effect, what Cities haue they en-
larged, and what Countries haue they enriched? [9]

Here is not only middle-class morality, thrift, and charity but
the inevitable emphasis on middle-class power. The state and
the king draw their strength from the merchant. And the
Court is an expensive brilliant ornament which the merchant
feels he can afford.

It is in the drama, always an index of popular feeling, that
the most important revelations of a middle-class psychology
are to be found. Despite Puritan objections the stage made a
powerful appeal to the citizens, who, it should be remembered,
had a rich tradition of playmaking and playgoing from the
heyday of the miracle and the morality. It should also be
remembered that Puritanism, as a clear-cut social and political
philosophy with broad citizen support, did not emerge until
well after the reign of Elizabeth and until such time as the
merchants and apprentices felt the need for a philosophical
basis in their opposition to the monarchy and the Established
Church. In the reign of Elizabeth countless citizens who, in
a few short years, were to clamor for the closing of the theatres, flocked to the Red Bull and the Fortune.

The Elizabethan theatre offered rich fare for the citizen.
Not only were plays with obvious domestic themes common
(such as *A Woman Killed with Kindness, Arden of Fe-*

[9] Nicholas Breton, *A Poste With A Packet of Mad Letters* (ed. 1633),
pp. 77–79.

versham, and the *Yorkshire Tragedy,* to name only the best known of the genre), but others dealing directly with the merchant in his favorite role as pillar of the state. Sir Thomas Gresham, the Merchant Prince, is the hero of Heywood's *If You Know Not Me, You Know Nobody* (1604–5). In *The Life and Death of Thomas, Lord Cromwell* (c. 1592) the hero is portrayed as the ideal citizen who never at the pinnacle of his fame forgets his origins in the middle class.

Of the plays glorifying the London tradesman perhaps Dekker's *The Shoemaker's Holiday* (1599) is the best example. Simon Eyre is the perfect type of citizen who, by dint of industry, piety, thrift, and good spirits, becomes Lord Mayor of London. Lacy, a nobleman, falls in love with the daughter of the Lord Mayor who preceded Simon in office, but class prejudice, which is quite as strong with the citizen as it is with Lacy's aristocratic kin, stays the match. The marriage and the happy ending to this pretty bit of class antagonism follows an appeal by the king himself to Simon and to the Earl of Lincoln, Lacy's uncle. Not only does Eyre refuse to regard himself as socially inferior to the Earl, he obviously approaches the king as man to man. Yet it is the king who finally reconciles the two. The king is the unifying symbol.

This antagonism between citizen and nobleman is expressed in various ways: directly, as in *The Shoemaker's Holiday,* and also in the social chasm between theatres attended almost exclusively by the citizens and the fashionable places patronized by gentlemen; indirectly, in the emphasis on solid citizen virtues, or the implied conviction that the state and the monarchy itself rested on the shoulders of the middle class. In the bourgeois drama of the Elizabethan period one is more aware of a positive statement of middle-class assumptions and convictions than of a negative hostility to the courtier. The citizen is too filled with his new importance as the backbone of the kingdom, too proud of his success, and above all too loyal to the state symbolized for him in the monarchy, to vent frequently his antagonism against the nobility. The sense of antagonism, though present and evident, is subordinate to a feeling of self-congratulation, and of loyalty to the monarchy which had made self-congratulation possible.

The one serious dramatic subject in which all Englishmen could rejoice was England—an England symbolized by the crown. Professor Schelling [10] has noted that one out of every five plays in the period of twenty years or so following the Spanish Armada was based on English history.

In the history plays more clearly than anywhere else one finds reflected the popular conceptions of the state and kingship, for though the dramatists were consistently royalists, so were the masses of the citizenry throughout the reigns of Elizabeth and James, and even in the early years of Charles. Nothing pleased the groundlings better than a royal king, and all were ready to approve sentiments expressing the subject's obligations of loyalty. In the portrayal of wicked and tyrannical kings, dramatists were careful to imply, and sometimes boldly to state, the contrast with the magnanimity of the reigning house. Plays about traitors, from *The Life and Death of Jack Straw* (1587) to Ford's *Perkin Warbeck* (1633), gave an opportunity for object lessons heartily approved by citizens, *for nothing was so objectionable to tradesmen as the disruptions of civil strife*. Strong kings were the favorite of the multitude. Thus it was not merely the clownery of Richard Tarlton in *The Famous Victories of Henry V* (c. 1586–88) which gave that play its popularity and paved the way for the long stage life of Shakespeare's great trilogy on Henry IV and Henry V. The glory of the Plantagenets was felt to forecast the parallel Tudor greatness. The Wars of the Roses, likewise important for stage purposes, represented to the Elizabethan chaos which the strong hands of Henry Tudor and his successors had modeled into the

[10] Felix E. Schelling, *Elizabethan Drama, 1558–1642*, I, 251–252.

state of their own time. Richard III with his crooked back and sinister record made an admirable stage foil for the noble founder of the House of Tudor, for whom the populace had an affection which made them never weary of plays magnifying Tudor grandeur.[11]

This vivid nationalism, this feeling of unity in the name of the crown, gave to Elizabethan literature its most inclusive and powerful symbolism—the "imperial theme." Royalism was the metaphor of the triumphant new England which had defeated feudal Spain and become a world power. Here was an image as rich and suggestive for the courtier as for the citizen. It stood for a fusion of values in letters, as it stood for a reconciliation of interests in society. But before dealing with the qualitative nature of this symbolism I must speak briefly of the class outlook of the Court in so far as it affected literature.

The courtier of this period was on the defensive. Not only was his power in the land threatened by the aspiring merchant, but also in order to maintain his position he was forced to adopt the merchant's practices, his way of life, and to an extent, therefore, his psychology.[12] No snob is so bitter as the snob who must imitate the object of his contempt. Whereas

[11] Wright, pp. 622–623.

[12] The commercial bias of the Elizabethan Court at a moment of great commercial opportunity transformed sections of the old nobility into "merchant adventurers," into a titled bourgeoisie. This process was encouraged by Elizabeth, who rewarded court favorites with trading monopolies. Both the commercially minded nobility and the middle class stood to profit from the encouragement which the monarchy gave to industry and trade in the days when there was urgent need to break the resistance of feudalism at home and abroad. In the Tudor period the middle class exerted little influence on the monarchy through Parliament, but for a time was content with the indirect backdoor "democracy" of its business dealing with Crown and Court. The Court remained in Elizabeth's time the decisive political interest in the kingdom, a Court bourgeois in its interests but aristocratic and absolutist in its composition and ideology.

the citizen, proud of his new importance, his new wealth, his new prestige in the eyes of the monarchy, was usually content to fear God, honor the king, and glorify his own virtues, —the courtier tended both to feel and to show resentment towards his upstart rival. As early as Peele's *Old Wives' Tale* (c. 1590), the aristocrat took public joy in ridiculing the citizen's somewhat illiterate taste in high romance. Beaumont and Fletcher's *Knight of the Burning Pestle* (1607-8) is perhaps the best known example of this type of satirical play. Middleton,[13] Brome, and others continued the tradition. In the seventeenth century, as the breach between Court and City widened, plays of a definite "class" nature became more frequent. The Court theatre delighted in accusing the citizen of all the vices from illiteracy to greed and cowardice.[14]

This bitterness, however, was poor enough compensation for the aggressive and even belligerent attitude of the middle class, reaching out for political as well as economic power now that the Elizabethan compromise was clearly over. The

[13] "Already in Middleton's drama the fashionable leisure class, which was to dominate later comedy so completely, assumes at times, through its crude but vigorous pressure on middle-class life, a social authority hitherto unrealized on the comic stage." [Kathleen Lynch, *The Social Mode of Restoration Comedy*, p. 28.]

[14] The final and utter cleavage between Court and City is realized in the reign of Charles I. The cultural life of the Court becomes completely isolated from the main currents of national life. A little coterie of poets and playwrights, including such men as D'Avenant, Carew, Waller, William Cartwright, Carlell, Montague, Lovelace, and Killigrew, wrote of "Platonic Love," a subject, indeed a fad, derived from D'Urfé, and imported by the French Queen Henrietta Maria. "Platonic" drama and Restoration comedy both depict small aristocratic social groups in which morals as well as manners have become regulated by an exacting social code (Kathleen Lynch, p. 79). As Alfred Harbage shows, the Cavalier plays "reveal a marked feminism" (*Cavalier Drama*, p. 39). The court drama was dominated by the Queen, whose tastes, though refined, were alien to the national tradition. Charles, retiring, even timid, inspired neither the imagination of his subjects nor the pens of his courtiers.

significant thing is that a decisive split in class relations, although foreshadowed in Elizabeth's reign, did not occur in a pronounced form until the characteristic nature of capitalist economy had fully revealed itself. In view of the *tension* in class relationships throughout the whole of Elizabeth's reign, the perishable nature of royalist symbolism is evident. I have stated that the courtier was forced to adopt, to an extent, the merchant's way of life, the merchant's psychology. Elizabeth's court was a court of Merchant Adventurers, of gentleman monopolists and projectors. The courtier's purse was as dear to him as his sword. He had deserted the lists for the market place. And yet poets like Spenser and Sidney are full of chivalric lore and on the surface at least seem to be writing in the best traditions of the feudal Court. Spenser seeks to revive Chaucerian English, and Sidney dies like a knight of old on a foreign strand. How could the richly allegorical *Faerie Queene* derive from "the merchant's psychology"? What possible relation has the refined literature of the Court with its heraldic pomp to the middle-class outlook? How does it reflect a new feeling for the monarchy, different, say, from Chaucer's feeling?

The answer is given by Elkin Wilson, who has written the most thorough and significant study yet attempted of royalist symbolism in the reign of Elizabeth:

The subjects of Queen Elizabeth had imaginations which were half mediaeval. Their fathers had been long accustomed to traditional symbols for social, political, and religious ideals. *Before those old symbols passed away the children warmed them into new and useful life.* If apprehended with sympathy, their use of a hallowed inheritance keeps a singular beauty for men who have other gods nearer to the mind's desire, if not always, perhaps, to the heart's.[15]

---

[15] *England's Eliza*, p. 1; italics mine.

In the poetry of Spenser one can see very clearly the use of old symbols for new purposes. Spenser uses mediaeval allegory "to fashion a gentleman or noble person in virtuous or gentle discipline." But the Spenserian knight is not the adulterous adventurer of old. He is a Puritan gentleman. That Spenser's social outlook is of the period of land enclosures and *laissez-faire* is seen by his portrait of Sir Artegall, who personifies Justice. I quote David Daiches:

> Sir Artegall's adventures are instructive, for they show us the other side of the idealist Elizabethan gentleman. But we have space only to refer to Sir Artegall's dealings with the giant whom he meets sitting on a rock preaching communism. The giant has "a huge paire of ballance in his hand" and he boasts:
>
> > That all the world he would weigh equallie,
> > If ought he had the same to counterpoys.
>
> As a result of his preaching equality "the vulgar did about him flock—in hope by him great benefit to gain," and this is too much for our noble knight, who reproaches the giant for endeavoring to weigh the world anew and "all things to an equal to restore." After an argument in which "the righteous Artegall" is unable to convince the giant that equality is wicked, he sends his iron-clad page Talus to cleave the giant from the rock and cast him into the sea (Artegall gets most of his dirty work done for him by Talus), and the poor giant is battered to pieces against the cliff before he falls in mangled fragments into the water. The deluded multitude show signs of resenting the death of their hero, whereupon Talus mows them down with his flail. Artegall, after watching Talus dispose of the "raskall rout" turns away and strolls to a neighboring castle for a refreshing cup of tea, or its Elizabethan equivalent.[16]

One is inevitably reminded of the fate of Winstanley's Diggers on St. George's Hill. As Daiches aptly points out, the Book on Justice reflects the attitude not only of the Court but also of the City to the ruthless imperialist subjugation of Ireland, Eng-

[16] *Literature and Society*, pp. 91–92.

land's first colony. In this courtly poem, with its feudal symbols and associations, the Puritan virtues are glorified—along with the imperialist aims of the Merchant Adventurer.

But a more subtle, and for my purposes, a more significant transformation of values is evident in *The Faerie Queene* and courtly literature in general. The symbol of royalism, clustered about with feudal references and habits of feeling and thinking, is charged with a new content and a new power.

As Wilson suggests, the Queen deliberately kept alive the mediaeval tradition of royal progresses, processions, and spectacles, a tradition which created a sort of resplendent intimacy between crown and subjects:

Englishmen felt that they were celebrating the waxing glory of their native land when they honoured their Deborah as she moved among them. They found no hospitality too rich for her. She represented the new greatness of their nation in its increasing consciousness of strength. Mere flattery and convention do not obscure the deepest notes heard in the progress and ballad verse. . . . Elizabeth knew that she was the happy personification of a happier nationality which her people were making articulate through their poets.[17]

The pageantry and splendor, full of reminiscences of a glorious past, of Richard the Lion-Hearted and the Crusades, of the Black Prince and the triumph over France, of the whole march of England and Englishmen to greatness and dignity, was identified with the person of the Queen, with Gloriana. Elizabeth was England.

From the popular broadside ballad to the poems of courtly homage this identification of Elizabeth with England takes on an almost mystical-religious suggestion. In the ballad "England's Lamentation For the late Treasons conspired against

[17] Wilson, p. 94.

the Queenes Maiestie by Frances Throgmorton: who was executed at Tyborne, on the 10th day of July, Anno 1584," England personified speaks:

> With brinishe teares, with sobbing sighes,
>   I, Englande, plunge in paine,
> To see and hear such secret sectes
>   amongst my people raine. . . .
> And where the Lord of Lords hath set,
>   his handmaide pure and cleene,
> Annoynting her my rightfull Prince,
>   to raigne a royall Queene:
> Inued with wisedome from above,
>   and storde with knowledge great,
> That flying Fame through all the world
>   her praises doth repeate. . . .
> Haue you not peace and plentie store,
>   which other realmes do want?
> Haue you not worldly pleasures more,
>   whereof there is not skant?
> Haue I not fostered you with foode,
>   which Nature yeelds not loth?
> Haue I not fed you dayntily
>   with milk and hony both? . . .
> And haue I not a carefull Prince,
>   and prop of all our stay,
> Which loueth me, which cares for you,
>   and prays for vs eche day? [18]

Here is Elizabeth, the anointed of God, the "prop of all our stay," against whose sovereignty only the basest villain might raise a hand. Her reign is guided by the wisdom of God. Indeed, the popular ballads are full of the idea that God had given England a strong Protestant Queen to save the country from the spreading contamination of papacy. The crown, as a symbol of unity, is sanctified by divine purpose. When the unhappy James wrote:

[18] *Broadside Blackletter Ballads,* pp. 21–23.

The state of monarchy is the supremest thing upon earth: for kings are not only God's lieutenants upon earth, and sit upon God's throne, but even by God himself they are called Gods . . .[19]

he was only carrying to an explicit conclusion (always a dangerous thing to do in England) the practical attitude of Elizabeth's subjects. But James was not Elizabeth, and the England of his reign was not the England of the 1580's. The difference is between an expanding, prosperous, and therefore unified nation, and a nation bewildered by the shock of depression and therefore divided by class antagonisms.[20] In this

[19] *Works,* p. 307.

[20] During the "boom" period following Drake's successful adventures in the New World (from about 1573 until the defeat of the Armada in 1588) there was comparative harmony between the capitalist courtier and his more humble rival of the city. But as early as 1597 a struggle began between Parliament and the Queen over the granting of monopolies to court favorites. The short-sighted mismanagement and get-rich-quick profiteering of the courtier-monopolists was upsetting English economy. In 1601 the Queen was forced to revoke several patents. However, the evils of monopoly were not solely responsible for the troubles that afflicted the last years of Elizabeth's reign. The court monopolist provided an apt target for the merchant citizen alarmed at the decrease in profits. But a new and fundamental phenomenon was appearing—the cycle of boom and depression. From 1586 on, England underwent a series of economic depressions, depressions which were to recur regularly and unavoidably in an economic system now identical with the international market. The citizen merchant attributed the economic distress to the system of court monopoly, and the attack on monopoly, which was to culminate in an attack on the monarchy itself, grew in volume and power throughout the reign of James. What was at first a resentment of favoritism and special privilege came to crystallize itself in terms of clear economic principles. In 1604, a Committee of the House of Commons reported: "All free subjects are born inheritable, as to their land, so also to the free exercise of their industry, in those trades whereto they apply themselves and whereto they live. Merchandise being the chief and richest of all other, and of greater extent and importance than all the rest, it is against the natural liberty of the subjects of England to restrain it into the hands of some few." (Ed. Gibson, *Codex Juria Ecclesiastici Anglicani,* 2nd ed., 1761, p. 1026. Quoted by Tawney, p. 166.) Here is economic individualism, or *laissez-faire,* becoming the articulate weapon of the middle classes in a struggle against the last vestiges of absolutist

ballad which I have quoted, so representative of popular feeling, the appeal in support of the Queen is not only to religion
and to nationalism, but to the well-filled stomach.

> Haue you not peace and plentie store
>   which other realmes do want? . . .
> Haue I not fostered you with foode,
>   which Nature yeelds not loth?
> Haue I not fed you dayntily
>   with milk and hony both?

It is not strange, perhaps, that when the land no longer flowed
with milk and honey the citizen began to doubt the identification of the crown with either God or the state.

The true nature of the theory of divine right, as a defense of
national stability against threatened disunion, was perhaps best
illustrated by the fact that it had little currency in England in
Tudor times. Despite differences between Calvinists and Anglicans
about the propriety of royal supremacy in the national church,
there was at no time prior to the death of Elizabeth any serious
threat to the internal peace and order of the kingdom. . . . The
actual stability and the unquestioned power of the Tudor monarchs made the theory of divine right unnecessary. The situation
changed in the seventeenth century when the outbreak of civil war
required both a defense of resistance on the ground of popular
right and a refutation of that position. The divine right of the king
then became a common position among the clerical apologists for
the Stuarts. However, the situations in France and England were
essentially different, because national sentiment in England was
at least as well represented by the judges of the common law or by
parliament as by the king. *The question was not national unity
against disunion, but what constitutional agent should stand for
national unity.*[21]

Surely it can be seen in this how a poet like Milton could be
rooted in English nationalism and patriotism, could be filled

power. From this point on, the middle-class acceptance of the monarchy
would be on middle-class terms, in accord with middle-class interests.

[21] G. H. Sabine, *A History of Political Thought,* p. 397; italics mine.

with the righteous zeal of a London shopkeeper, the knight-errantry of a Sidney, the adventurous romantic imperialism of a Drake, and the cold-blooded imperialism of a Spenser, how he could be immersed in the sights and sounds and colors of a great poetic tradition still warm and near, and yet be so far from the centre and spring of the tradition as to miss it entirely. "What constitutional agent should stand for national unity?" That question would have amazed and horrified Sidney and Spenser, just as it would have amazed and horrified Dekker and Heywood and the ballad-mongers of the London streets. But in Milton's time this question was on every man's lips, and Milton himself answered it—against the king.

Elizabeth needed no theory of divine right to maintain her hold on the people, but imaginatively, in the symbolism of her poets she was a "Heauenlie Goddesse," a divinity. I have quoted above from the broadside ballads because I feel that the popular poetry of the time shows more directly, less subtly, the association of religious, political, and economic ideas in the veneration of the Queen. There is no essential disagreement between the purport of the Throgmorton ballad and the court poems of praise. In the court poems, however, there is evident a qualitative difference, revealing not merely a greater sophistication, greater skill at versification, but a different social, and consequently, a different artistic heritage. The author of the Throgmorton ballad sees God directing the affairs of England through an able lieutenant. The arrangement is to the profit of everyone, and blast the wretch who interferes! This was the clear-cut, comfortable, devoted, but devoted-because-it pays loyalty of George a Greene.

But in the literature of the Court one can see clearly the transformation of the feudal values, a phenomenon which I mentioned earlier. True, mediaeval pageantry was put on display for the people as a whole, but at the Court the cult of chivalry was actually practised, and in high seriousness. The gentlemen of the time may have soiled their ruffs, but they still wore them. The aristocracy still venerated as an ideal the traditional "conception of a true knight as an educated gentleman who serves his prince and state and rises by his worth and noble deeds to an immortality of fame." [22] As I have pointed out, this idealism was not always realized in an ennobling fashion. The temptations of a profit-seeking world were often too much for this saintly code. Perhaps it is significant that Spenser sees no contradiction between Sir Artegall and the ethic of a mediaeval world, the world which provides so much of the poem's flesh if so little of its spirit. The heritage of the Romance of the Rose, of the feudal tournament and joust, of the splendor and pomp of the baronial hall, is moulded un-selfconsciously and without deliberate effort into a glorification of a monarch who, in fact, symbolized the death of the whole baronial-chivalric tradition. For instance, the knightly veneration of the lady as goddess is transformed easily enough into a royal salute:

> And well beseemes all knights of noble name,
> That covett in th' immortall booke of fame
> To be eternized, that same to haunt,
> And doen their service to that soveraigne dame,
> That glory does to them for guerdon graunt:
> For she is heavenly borne, and heaven may justly vaunt.[28]

What is even more significant is the way in which the cult of the Virgin Mary is carried over into the cult of the Virgin Queen. The mediaeval convention of service to the lady and above all to the Virgin Lady brought to the new poetic sym-

[22] Wilson, p. 172.
[28] *The Faerie Queene,* I. x. 59.

bolism of royalty rich overtones and suggestions from the past.

As Wilson points out, in John Dowland's *The Second Book of Songs or Airs* (1600), "There are verses that suggest an actual substitution of the English virgin for the Catholic in the hearts of ardent Protestant knights." I shall quote one stanza:

> When others sing *Venite exultemus!*
> Stand by, and turn to *Noli emulari!*
> For *Quare fremuerunt,* use *Oremus*
> *Vivat ELIZA!* for an *Ave MARI!*
> And teach those swains that live about thy cell;
> To sing *Amen,* when thou dost pray so well! [24]

This theme, crudely stated here, runs like a thread through court poetry and drama, binding Elizabethan literature to the most vivid conventions of the middle ages, yet permitting new directions, new aspirations, the full expression of a new spirit which defied the content if not the form of the past.

And so with pageantry and tournaments, with the encouragement of the chivalric cult, Elizabeth held in loyalty to herself and to her once precarious throne elements which might easily have been turned to the disruption of her state.

I think it obvious that the Queen alone could not have effected this harmony, and that a James, even with the arts of an archangel, would have failed to maintain it. The forces of disharmony, apparent even in those "few fortunate years," could not be checked by charm or diplomacy once the storm was up. True, James had neither charm nor diplomacy, and Elizabeth had something of one and much of the other. The historical accident of her personality and of her well-advertised virginity, left a deep impression on the kind and form of

[24] John Dowland, *The Second Book of Songs or Airs* (1600). Quoted by Wilson, p. 206.

culture in her day. But the class alliance which she manipulated and managed so skillfully was not of her making, and its destruction was foreshadowed before it occurred.

Meanwhile, for literature, two important streams had converged and coalesced. This happened because of the vitality of those subterranean urgencies which set the direction. The pride of the citizen in his own class was accompanied by a devotion to the monarchy which had aided and abetted him in his rise to prominence. The pride of the courtier in his class traditions was accompanied by a devotion to the monarchy which encouraged him to repair his feudal fortunes in the capitalist market. The citizen brought to literature a direct, healthy, democratic sense of familiarity with kingship. The courtier brought the glamour of the past renewed for a happy instant in the reality of the present. Qualitatively, at its highest point in the work of Shakespeare, Elizabethan literature absorbed both streams.

Henry V, Shakespeare's ideal king, is at once the "parfait gentil knight" of the courtly tradition and the popular leader of men quite at home with the yeomen of his army. The battle of Agincourt is won by the common soldier led by a king with the common touch. The speech in which Henry woos Katherine is typical of him:

Marry, if you would put me to verses, or to dance for your sake, Kate, why you undid me: for the one, I have neither the words nor measure. I have no strength in measure, yet a reasonable measure in strength. If I could win a lady by leap-frog, or by vaulting into my saddle with my armour on my back, under the correction of bragging be it spoken, I should quickly leap into a wife. Or if I might buffet for my love, or bound my horses for her favours, I could lay on like a butcher and sit like a jack-an-napes, never off. But before God, Kate, I cannot look greenly nor gasp out my eloquence, nor have I no cunning in protestation; only downright oaths, which I will never use till urged, nor will never break for urging. If thou canst love a fellow of this temper, Kate, whose face is not worth sun-burning, that never looks in his glass for love of anything he sees there, let thine eye be thy cook. I speak to thee plain soldier. . . . . And while thou livest, dear Kate, take a fellow of plain and uncoined constancy, for he perforce must do thee right, because he hath not the gift to woo in other places; for these fellows of infinite tongue, that can rime themselves into ladies' favours, they do always reason themselves out again.[25]

This is the love-making of the soldier-citizen. It expressly scorns the pretty euphuism of the Court. And yet Henry is a courtier. Or, I should say, he is more than a courtier just as he is more than a citizen—a fusion of both—and thus the perfect symbol of unity and order. Shakespeare's idea of kingship is made to appeal to both dominant classes. Perhaps Wilson Knight has the most pertinent word to say on this problem of royal symbolism in Shakespeare:

Kingship must be related closely to "order." Now this concept is of profound importance in Shakespeare. Most of the history plays and many of the tragedies present a plot of conflict and disorder. Disorder in man, party, or state is a recurring theme. It is often related to images of "disease." Sometimes we find concise disorder-symbolism to direct our understanding: weird phenomena in sky or earth foretelling change and disaster. . . . Now the king is himself an order-symbol, being both heart and head of the organic body of the state. Thus a close attention to the exceeding importance of his kings, and continued emphasis on fidelity and allegiance as the purest forms of "honour," and the consequent hatred of treachery, seen in an extreme instance in the plot against Henry V, where it is shown to merit sixty-five lines of vigorous and withering reproof prior to the offenders' execution. By viewing the king as a symbol of order we may often focus in the individual speech, act, or play a more than local and individual significance.[26]

The crown symbolizes the unity of the nation. But the symbol is often presented as an ideal which contrasts with a

[25] *Henry V*, V. ii. 135 ff.
[26] *The Imperial Theme*, pp. 6–7.

less than ideal reality. Shakespeare does not slight the weakness of John and Lear. Like the authors of *Gorbuduc* he fears the recurrence of civil strife, the shape of things to come. Sometimes he juxtaposes the semi-divine symbol and the unworthy or unsuccessful king, as in Richard II's speech:

> Not all the water in the rough rude sea
> Can wash the balm off from an anointed king;
> The breath of worldly men cannot depose
> The deputy elected by the Lord.[27]

And sometimes he makes the king himself aware of his shortcomings:

> Poor naked wretches, whereso'er you are,
> That bide the pelting of this pitiless storm,
> How shall your houseless heads and unfed sides,
> Your loop'd and window'd raggedness, defend you
> From seasons such as these? O, I have ta'en
> Too little care of this! Take physic, pomp;
> Expose thyself to feel what wretches feel,
> That thou mayst shake the superflux to them
> And show the heavens more just.[28]

"Take physic, pomp." Shakespeare's ideal king is not merely splendid. As Knight points out:

Henry V is the Messiah of true kingliness. He is both wholly responsive to the divine responsibility he holds and also wholly glorified by temporal success. The others often possessed the "ceremony" without the soul of kingship. He has both in full measure. And even he feels wearied by the burden of his responsibility: yet, because he knows that "ceremony" is but a poor requital for his infinite anxiety, because he is the soul of "honour" and "warriorship," because he ever puts faith in God, he is shown as a perfect king. There are no short-cuts to kingly peace in Shakespeare. It will be clear, then, that the world-glory of kingship, the "tide of

---

[27] *Richard II*, III. ii. 54.
[28] *King Lear*, III. iv. 28.

pomp" on which it puts to sea, is both a positive good and a potential lure to evil and disorder. Joined to essential wisdom and integrity, it is one aspect of a high ideal; divorced from those, it is an unreality, a tinsel thing of tawdriness for which rash men sacrifice the order of nations. . . . *World-glory is endued with imaginative splendour as the sign and emblem of greatness. But it remains an emblem.*[29]

Shakespeare can draw on the knightly tradition in portraying the king or prince:

> I saw young Harry with his beaver on,
> His cuisses on his thighs, gallantly arm'd,
> Rise from the ground like feather'd Mercury,
> And vaulted with such ease into his seat,
> As if an angel dropp'd down from the clouds,
> To turn and wind a fiery Pegasus,
> And witch the world with noble horsemanship.[30]

But the king without the sober responsible virtues of the citizen is only a glittering shell, a menace to the state. A king must justify his rank. He must provide and maintain the unity and oider necessary to the healthy nation.

I have not the space here to discuss in detail Shakespeare's treatment of royalist imagery in all its aspects. Both Knight and Miss Spurgeon support me in my contention that the connotation of majesty in Shakespeare is always positive. To be "every inch a king" is the *summum bonum,* even though the individual king may fall short of the ideal. It should be noticed here that "gold" and "ceremony," often associated with kingship in Shakespeare, are not consistently employed as symbols of worth. "Gold," precious stones, the forces of nature, all appear at times to adorn the praise of love, virtue, and kingliness. But they are not in themselves positive in-

[29] Knight, pp. 7–8; italics mine.
[30] *I Henry IV,* IV: i. 104.

clusive symbols. Romeo's speech to the apothecary is a clear example:

> There is thy gold—worse poison to men's souls,
> Doing more to murther in this loathsome world,
> Than these poor compounds that thou mayst not sell.
> I sell thee poison; thou hast sold me none.[31]

Majesty for Shakespeare has a quality of inwardness. It is spiritual as well as worldly:

> My crown is in my heart, not on my head;
> Not deck'd with diamonds and Indian stones,
> Nor to be seen. My crown is called content;
> A crown it is that seldom kings enjoy.[32]

Compact in the concept of kingship are the knightly qualities of Arthur, of the Spenserian romance, the almost religious veneration of the Court poets in love with their Virgin Queen, and the homely familiarity of George a Greene. Royalist symbolism in Shakespeare draws its life from both Court and City, and from the role which the Tudor monarchy has played in effecting unity.

It is significant, too, that Henry V, the monarch who crushes feudal reaction, is represented as the perfect king. This play is the climax of the series of chronicles glorifying the growth of England to full nationhood. Here the ideal symbol and the man approximate each other. It is the height of Shakespeare's optimism. In the tragedies Shakespeare wrestles with the conflict of the ideal and the real. His royalist symbolism remains positive—but more urgent. In *Lear,* for instance, the king is not worthy of his crown and the kingdom is brought to ruin. Weakness has permitted the release of feudal forces of disorder. There is hope at the end—in Edgar and Albany—but

---

[31] *Romeo and Juliet*, V. i. 80.
[32] *3 Henry VI*, III. i. 62.

the triumphant sense of "All's well with the world" which pervaded *Henry V* is never recaptured. In the great tragedies one is conscious of a profound conflict of the ideal and the real—and "all but inmost faith is overthrown." [33]

While Shakespeare was writing his last plays a new concept of royalty was winning favor in the theatre. I have mentioned the growing tendency of Court writers in the early seventeenth century to ridicule the citizen. This tendency corresponded to the widening split in class relations, the opposition of the merchant to the court monopoly, and the waning power of the throne as a progressive, unifying factor in

[33] Both C. J. Sisson ("The Mythical Sorrows of Shakespeare," in *Proceedings of the British Academy*, XX [1934], pp. 45–71) and R. W. Chambers ("The Jacobean Shakespeare and *Measure for Measure*," *Proceedings of the British Academy*, XXIII [1937], pp. 135–193) attack the notion that Shakespeare's tragedies reflect (a) personal sorrow, (b) pessimism over the state of the nation under James. To quote Sisson: "The whole notion that the early years of the reign of James were years of cynicism and disillusionment is a feat of the delusive imagination, working backwards from a knowledge of the breakdown of the Stuart monarchy under Charles" (p. 55). There can be no doubt that James was at first a popular figure. Nor can there be any doubt that the royalist symbolism of the great tragedies is positive. I would not suggest that the later plays are cynical or disillusioned. Certainly it would be unsafe to attribute Shakespeare's sense of tragedy to questionable "facts" of his personal experience. As there is no biography of Shakespeare there can be no convincing biographical criticism of his work. However I must insist that the royalist symbol in Shakespeare is of Tudor-Elizabethan inspiration, that in his Jacobean plays the royalist ideal is usually presented in conflict with the real, that in the drama of the Jacobean period the royalist symbol loses much of its Elizabethan suggestiveness (see text above), and that "the breakdown of the Stuart monarchy under Charles" was foreshadowed by the growing urgency of capitalist crisis in the reign of James (a phenomenon which had troubled the last years of Elizabeth herself). Despite the popularity of Prince Henry (and to a lesser degree of James himself), social unity was breaking under the stress of economic forces. Kings more diplomatic and more gifted in the arts of popularity than James or Charles might have prevented civil war, but only by acquiescing in the rising demands of the middle class, and by admitting that the traditional conception of kingship was an anachronism. The Elizabethan royalist symbol was *Elizabethan*.

society. Along with this satirical drama came a crop of plays glorifying monarchy, but in a fashion alien to the Shakespearian tradition. The King in Beaumont and Fletcher's *Maid's Tragedy* [34] is a dissolute wretch, but above criticism because he is king. The King in the same men's *A King and No King* ardently seeks to commit incest. Fletcher's Loyal Subject is a servile creature who submits to endless indignities at the hands of a king, and for his patience is rewarded finally by the king's favor. It is almost as if the court dramatists sought to defy bourgeois morality with their degenerate wastrel kings who could do no wrong no matter how desperately they might try. The "divine right" of these monarchs was the divine right to disregard responsibility and censure.

Shakespeare's ideal monarch had divinity in him, a divinity created in the image of the people. Beaumont and Fletcher wrote in self-conscious defiance of the city. Their work not only represented the rejection of a cultural tradition in which courtly and bourgeois values had merged. It also represented the disintegration of the courtly tradition itself. I have stressed the importance of the Elizabethan class alliance for the transformation of feudal values into vital new symbols. The cult of chivalry, Virgin-worship, even the legend of Arthur were given fresh validity. There was a qualitative change of values within the old forms. But with the ripening of class hostility, with the failure of the monarchy to continue its progressive and unifying function, this magic ceased. Class-consciousness begat a self-consciousness. The great theme of nationhood, of

[34] The dramatic conflict in the typical Beaumont and Fletcher play was between love and duty, a theme which anticipated the "heroic drama" of the Restoration. This concept of "duty"—to the state, to the king—was not new. Indeed, it was central in Shakespeare. But in Beaumont and Fletcher it becomes a conventional abstraction because the royalist symbol to which it is attached has lost its vitality.

progress, of unity, was lost, replaced by a decadent itch for thrills. The endless plays dealing with incest, sex-crimes, and refined torture indicate more than writer's cramp. The courtier found Lucrezia Borgia more attractive than the Faerie Queene. A great tradition was dying. On this point both citizen and courtier would have cordially agreed.

Nevertheless the courtier continued to write of kings, splendid, ornamental, corrupt, ruling by the grace of God. Indeed, after the first fury of the Court's antagonism to the City had spent itself, something of dignity if not vitality returned to the *courtly* conception of royalty. One feels this in the writings and speeches of Strafford, in the sermons of John Donne, and in the pale idealism of the Cavalier poets. But royalism as an inclusive touchstone of values was lost forever. The royalist symbol did not survive the reign of James.

The short period of relief that followed his [James's] succession in 1603 gave way almost at once to a feeling of uncertainty and danger even greater than that of the last years of Elizabeth. His personal unpopularity as a sovereign went some way to bring this about. The lowering of the standards in the court was immediate; slackness of discipline, loss of dignity and increase of expense combined to produce at once dissatisfaction and a feeling of unsteadiness. Plots to depose him broke out again almost at once; Cobham's in November 1603 involved Raleigh, a man who still represented the Elizabethans in the eyes of some of his contemporaries, and the Gunpowder Plot in November 1605, which only just missed its mark, would have left the country deprived at one blow of all its leaders, temporal and ecclesiastical, and all the machinery of state.[35]

The shattering of the royalist symbol in the vise of history meant, more than anything else, the dissociation of those inward and external qualities which had coalesced in the

[35] U. Ellis-Fermor, *The Jacobean Drama*, p. 3.

Shakespearian image. I have noted how religious values were drawn into the veneration of the Queen. Not only were traditional Catholic forms of worship transformed into the worship of Elizabeth, but also the Hebraic concept of the King of Kings was easily visualized by the Elizabethan. Religious "picture-thinking" in the orthodox monarchical forms was inevitable in an age when the ruler, by common consent, was "Heauenlie Borne," and guided in her every deed by the Lord of Hosts. The following is typical of popular feeling as to the almost family relation of King of Kings and Queen of England:

> Your owne experience sheweth that no practize will preuaile to harme one hair of hir head whome next God you hate most; for the Lorde of hostes doth keepe hir, he hath set legions of angels about hir, they march with hir, they goe before hir, and garde hir from all treasons.[36]

The Hebrew God provided Elizabeth with a personal bodyguard. For both courtier and citizen the Queen was the manifestation of heavenly splendor. As Wilson puts it, "Religious patriotism—or patriotic religion—unites Deloney with Sir John Davies in hymns to this queen who is preserved by God to bring peace and to save 'Pure Religion.' "[37]

Well into the seventeenth century John Donne, among others, continues the religious picture-thinking of the Elizabethans. In a sermon preached at Whitehall, November 2, 1617, he says: "Though as Princes are Gods, so their well-govern'd courts are copies and representations of Heaven; yet the copy cannot be better than the original."[38] In another

---

[36] Henri Estienne, *The Stage of Popish toyes: . . .* compyled by G. N. [George North], 1581, sig. M 4. Quoted by Wilson, p. 225.
[37] P. 226.
[38] *Donne,* p. 172.

sermon he selects those biblical manifestations of God which have courtly associations:

As God has spangled his firmaments with stars, so hath he his scriptures with names, and metaphors and denotations of power. Sometimes he shines out in the name of a *Sword,* and of a *Target,* and of a *Wall,* and of a *Tower,* and of a *Rocke,* and of a *Hill;* and sometimes in that glorious and manifold constellation of all together, *Dominus exercituum, The Lord of Hosts.* God as God, *is never represented to us with Defensive Armes.*[39]

This feudal strain is mingled appropriately enough with a solid imperialist sense. In a sermon to members of the Virginia Plantation Company in 1622 he says:

You shall make this Island, which is but as the suburbs of the old world, a Bridge, a Gallery to the new; to join all to that world that shall never grow old, the Kingdome of heaven. You shall add persons to this Kingdome and to the Kingdome of heaven, and add names to the Bookes of our Chronicles, and to the Book of Life.[40]

Donne shares with courtier and citizen an enthusiasm for wealth and outward splendor. "Riches is the metaphor in which the Holy Ghost hath delighted to express God and heaven to us." [41] He quotes from scripture to prove that God is pictured with gold and jewels, never in the clothing of the poor. Here, too, is an argument for worldly wealth. "And therefore labour we all earnestly in the ways of some lawfull calling, that we may have our portion of this world by good meanes." [42]

Sound bourgeois doctrine. Indeed, this is a typical Puritan sermon. Donne, then, does manage to bring together courtly

[39] *Donne,* pp. 135–136; italics mine in the final sentences.
[40] *Donne,* p. 54.
[41] *Donne,* p. 76.
[42] *Donne,* p. 77.

imagery and bourgeois values. God still looks rather like the
King of England. The destiny of England is still intertwined
with the destiny of heaven. This may seem on the face of it
to contradict my previous statement that Elizabethan royalist
symbolism was shattered by the growing class division of the
Jacobean period. Certainly royalism in Donne is not the
tawdry blatant thing that it is in Beaumont and Fletcher. It
is only natural that the dignity of a tradition should cling
to the pulpit after it had deserted the theatre. It is also significant that Donne's admiration of royalty seems to derive
from his admiration of Elizabeth. He usually flatters James
in terms of a reference to his great predecessor. "And to a
higher comparison, than to her, I know not how to carry it." [43]
He clinches an argument in favor of the equality of women
by pointing to Queen Elizabeth "as scarce any former king
hath equalled." [44] One suspects that Donne's royalism is
nostalgic. During his last years as Dean he seems more and
more inclined to subordinate the pomp and power of kings
to abstract ideas of justice and righteousness. I shall quote
from a late sermon, which reflects the waning ardor for kings
of an Elizabethan who had lived through to the edge of the
Civil Wars:

Heires of the joy, and heires of the glory of heaven; where if
thou lookest down, and see kings fighting for crownes, thou canst
look off as easily as from boys at stool-ball for points here. And
from kings triumphing after victory, as easily, as a Philosopher
from a Pageant of children here. Where thou shalt not be *subject
to any other title of Dominion in others, but Jesus of Nazareth,
King of the Jews, nor ambitious of any other title in thy selfe, but
that which thou possesseth, to be the childe of God.*[45]

[43] *Donne*, p. 57.
[44] *Donne*, pp. 106–118.
[45] *Donne*, p. 222; italics mine.

This heaven in which one escapes the dominion of lordly rank is emphatically not the heaven so like the Court of England which Donne had once imagined. Even in Donne, the court preacher, inward religious values and royalist pictorial values were forced apart.

In the sermons of the less courtly preachers this dissociation of values had come earlier and more decisively. Says Thomas Taylor, a master of Puritan rhetoric:

> Men cast up their heads, and look aloft, if they be Lords of some small Manour, or possession; but to be a King or Prince of a peece of earth, lifting them in their conceits above the tops of the clouds: But a poore Christian is better contented with poore and naked Christ.[46]

As the king no longer symbolizes a unified nation he can no longer symbolize a universal god. The Baptists, the Quakers, and the other sects of the common people came to make a sharp distinction between the King of Heaven and the kings of the earth:

> In the Kingdomes of men some have greater estates than others and are in higher honours and authority; and this breeds envy and emulation and strife and distance, etc. but in the Son's Kingdome . . . all that are counted worthy to dwell therein do alike inherit all things.[47]

The Son is still "King" in the writings both of the common people and of the court preachers, but the nature and the appearance of his kingship vary with the social aspirations of the men who take his name. The word "king" no longer connotes a value which all men can readily understand. In the

[46] "The Pearl of the Gospel," in Taylor, *Three Treatises,* pp. 18–19. Quoted in Haller, *The Rise of Puritanism,* p. 159.
[47] *Select Works of William Dell,* London (1773), p. 177. Quoted in G. H. Sabine's *Winstanley,* Introduction.

writings of the Puritans and the sectaries it becomes disem-
bodied, abstract. In the courtly writings it is too patently associated with the King of England, and its emotive appeal is
thus limited to the court.

The work of the Cambridge Platonists demonstrates how
completely the pictorial symbol of kingliness lost its religious
significance in the seventeenth century. God, for John Smith
is not a princely lawgiver, but

the Eternal Reason, that Almighty Mind and Wisdom which our
understandings converse with; but he is also that unstained Beauty
and Supreme Good which our Wills are perpetually catching after.

God is but One, he and his Name One . . . and where we find
Wisdom, Justice, Loveliness, Goodness, Love and. Glory in their
highest elevations and most unbounded dimensions, That is He.[48]

Heaven is not a royal court but "happiness." The entire pictorial mythology, not only of Elizabethan literature and
Anglican sermonizing, but of the Bible itself, is abandoned.
The philosophical concept is substituted for the regal portrait. Basil Willey [49] attributes this rational trend in theology
to the growing influence of scientific thought, in particular
to the influence of Descartes. Certainly the scientific revolution was in rapid progress and is in reality one phase of the
upheaval in European culture which I have noted in social
and economic terms. The old mythology could no more withstand the assault of scientific thinking than absolute monarchy could withstand the middle-class revolution. But when
one observes the degradation of the royalist symbol in
seventeenth-century drama, and the rejection of royalism in
the religious writings of Platonists and Baptists alike, one is
aware of a phenomenon more inclusive than the influence

[48] *Discourse,* John Smith (1673 edition), I, p. 132.
[49] *The Seventeenth Century Background,* pp. 137 ff.

of Descartes. A once self-sufficient universe of values was gone from the thinking and feeling of Englishmen.

Milton, then, came late to his praise of England and his praise of God. A new spirit, bred of class war and nourished by the Scriptures, gave sinew and purpose to his work. But even in his use of the Hebraic mythology, he could not escape the problem of communication created by the changed connotation of the royalist symbol. The Hebraic and Elizabethan image of God and King had been too closely interchanged to be easily distinct now. Ornamental royalist values proper to epic grandeur retained a sensuous fascination for Milton, and, of course, they had the sanction of epic tradition. But royalist imagery could no longer communicate the social and psychological virtues. A complex poetic symbolism had become a kind of interior decoration. Milton's poetic aim demanded a sensuous style. He could not follow John Smith into abstractions. He consciously adopted the literary conventions of the Renaissance. And he was caught fast in one of the most perplexing dilemmas in the history of poetry.

II

The Problem of the Early Poems
and the Early Plans

It is not to be expected that the young Milton of the Cambridge and Horton years, absorbed in his studies both academic and private, cushioned by a generous allowance from his father, and quite isolated in fact and thought from the busy practical world in which that allowance was earned, could realize in clear terms the social and cultural rift which was dividing England. At Cambridge he was to toughen his intellectual muscles in the fight against the mediaeval system of education, and announce himself the champion of the modern scientific outlook. In his *Third Prolusion, Contra Philosophiam Scholasticam,* he argues:

How much better would it be and more worthy of you as members of this University to study all the countries of the world set out in the map and to visit them in your imagination, to scan the places trodden by the heroes of old, to traverse too the regions glorified in the tales of famous poets, now to cross the stormy Adriatic, now to approach unhurt the flames of Etna; next to observe the manners of men and the national governments that have been fairly ordered, and thence to investigate the nature of all living things, descending from them to study the hidden properties of stones and plants. And do not hesitate to soar into the heavens; and then gaze on all the varied shapes of the clouds, the mass of snow collected there, and the place from which the dews of morning spring. Then look into the coffers where the hail is kept, and examine all the stores of thunderbolts. And do not be baffled by what Jupiter or Nature mean when a huge dreadful comet keeps threatening the heaven with conflagration; and do not miss one of the whole number of even the tiniest stars that are scattered between the poles.[1]

This is a good enough statement of the Baconian position. Mr. Tillyard suggests that it may reflect "the popular science of Sylvester's DuBartas." [2] The significant thing about this and other attacks which Milton made on the mediaevalism of Cambridge is the enthusiasm with which he championed a cause already won on the main front, the zeal with which he tilted at vanishing windmills. In a sense Milton was fortunate in Cambridge. The English universities were the last strongholds of intellectual reaction. Here, and perhaps only here, the young rebel could get the scent of the old battle in his nostrils, could go forth and slay the feudal dragon for the glory of the brave new world. In this dusty bypath of learning one could feel the thrill of heresy in reading Spenser and Sidney, Ovid and Virgil.[3] To proclaim an interest in government, in science, and in geography was to issue a manifesto with the pride of a revolutionist. The intellectual weapons of the Renaissance came fresh and exciting to Milton's hand, and he used them as though they had never been used before —in grimmer and more decisive battles. In other words, Milton participated in the last phase of the war against mediaevalism, that one which finally involved the academic backwash of culture.

While John Donne in the *Anniversaries* and Browne in the *Urn Burial* saw disintegration and smelt decay in nature it-

[1] *S.M.*, p. 1106.

[2] *Milton*, p. 16, n.

[3] This is not, of course, meant as a slight. Milton's deliberate attack on the Cambridge curriculum was a healthy thing. In this stage of his development "the cultural lag" worked to Milton's advantage, enabling him to live in the immediate past without any conscious sense of "escape." At Cambridge the immediate past was in advance of the present.

self (just as Henry Adams was to do in a later but not dis-similar period of confusion and relapse), Milton inclined eagerly to the most advanced and optimistic of Renaissance ideas. In the Latin poem *Naturam non pati Senium* he pro-claimed the vigor and expansiveness of nature, anticipating the eighteenth century philosophy of progress.[4] How com-pletely he was to reject his own early optimism I shall discuss in a later chapter. Despair with society was one day to breed in Milton a more universal despair. It should be noted here that there is no reason to suspect that Milton's rejection of the pessimism of Donne and the others involved in it any understanding of the social and economic confusion which determined that pessimism. The disintegration of the Eliza-bethan cultural synthesis, the wrenching apart of courtly and bourgeois values, moved Donne and his generation to feel that society was "all in peeces, all cohaerance gone, All just supply, and all relation." Milton's early controversies (as recorded in the *Prolusions*) show him completely unaffected by (because unaware of) the frustration of the late Eliza-bethans. Thanks to the anachronism of the university Milton began where they began, championing causes which they had already won—and lost. In the formative years, then, human-ism is as new and intense for Milton as it might have been for the first pupil of Erasmus. It is for a "first-nighter" that "frenzied Tragedy shakes her blood-stained sceptre." Neither the social chasm which was dividing the London theatre against itself, nor the crabbed Puritanism which was attack-ing the theatre from the pulpit, is reflected in Milton's youth-ful enthusiasm for the drama.[5] In the "finely hybrid culture"

[4] English translation in *S.M.*, pp. 100–101.
[5] For a full account of Milton's interest in the drama see Ida Langdon, *Milton's Theory of Poetry and the Fine Arts,* Chap. IV.

of Milton's student years, classical, Elizabethan, and Puritan elements were held in suspension *in Milton's mind if not in Milton's world*. In the Latin *Elegy I,* for instance, there is not only a show of interest in Elizabethan tragedy, but also a happy fusion of Ovidizing love poetry with the typical citizen's praise of London, reminiscent of the Elizabethan ballad:

Let not the Tarpeian Muse boast of Pompey's colonnade and of the theatre full of Ausonian stoles. It is to the maids of England that the foremost glory is due; let it be enough for thee, foreign woman, to be able to follow after. And thou, oh city of London, built by Dardanian settlers, conspicuous far and wide for thy turreted head, thou, fortunate to excess, dost enclose within thy walls all the beauty that the pendent earth possesses. Not so many are the stars that sparkle in thy clear air, hosts that attend upon Endymion's goddess, as are the maidens that, conspicuous for golden beauty, move through thy streets, a radiant throng to see. Men believe that to this spot came life-giving Venus herself, drawn by her twin doves, with her quivered soldier close to her side, ready to rank this city above Cnidos.[6]

And mingled almost playfully with this "pretty piece of paganism" is the Puritan note. "But I, while the indulgent mood of the blind boy permits, am preparing to leave these happy precincts with all convenient speed, and to keep far away from the ill-famed halls of treacherous Circe."[7] Years later Milton expressed regret for the frivolous pagan quality of some of the Latin poems. But in the early poems, even in *Elegy VI,* the poem in which he dedicates himself to the serious epic, and announces in pious tones that he is "hymning the king of heavenly lineage, prince of peace,"[8] he shows no moral repulsion for the specifically pagan. The serious

[6] *S.M.,* p. 86.
[7] *S.M.,* p. 86.
[8] *S.M.,* pp. 91–92.

poet must live seriously and austerely for the sake of his *poetry*. The composer of "light Elegy" has his place too, and to him "bountiful feasts are *permitted,* and frequent draughts of wine." Milton vows a stricter life than this because his poetry is to have a different and nobler function. He concluded the *Elegy VII* [9] with a half-hearted frown for his "folly," his "ill-directed zeal" in writing what is certainly an extremely sensuous poem. But he has written it—and has thoroughly enjoyed himself. An exquisite classical sense of hedonism was to remain with Milton until the last bitter days. It achieves fine expression in the sonnet *To Mr. Lawrence,* in the *Areopagitica,* and in *Paradise Lost* itself. At no time does Milton suffer from the conviction of guilt characteristic of Puritans like Baxter and Bunyan. It is perhaps no accident that the obsession with the "sinful" past is more common among the Puritan converts from the lower middle class and the working class, men who received the doctrine in a single unmixed draught, than among young men of Milton's class and training, heirs of all the ages because still untouched by their own.

In another and perhaps more important respect the hybrid nature of Milton's early interests showed itself. Classicism not only gave flesh to the spirit, it kept alive for the university men literary conventions already dead on the London streets.

The Roman poets are all devoted to liturgy, Ovid no less than the rest. In their spirit, Milton dedicates a poem of lament to each of two lately deceased bishops, poems of a reverential cast, suggestive of solemn choirs, sacred lights, and a stately apostolic succession. Just look at the ancient magic! The fact that a Bishop had died would not ordinarily induce a youth of Puritan tendencies to grace his obsequies with a poem; but if the youth is also a disciple of Ovid and Horace, casting about for a meet subject for ode or

[9] *S.M.,* pp. 92–94.

elegy, he might, without straining conscience, devote a Latin lament to the distinguished man, Bishop though he be.[10]

In the same year (1626) that he wrote the elegy *On the
Death of the Bishop of Winchester,* his interest in the classical
epic led him to compose *In Quintum Novembris,* a poem on
the Gunpowder Plot in which the figure of King James is
given epic proportions, not because of any profound feeling
for the Stuarts, but because of the machinery borrowed from
classical literature, and, perhaps, from the *Locustae* of Phineas
Fletcher.[11]

Later in this chapter I shall discuss more fully Milton's treatment of James in the various poems on the Gunpowder Plot.
My point here is that Milton's eclectic and detached culture
was for a few impressionable years susceptible to a wide variety
of literary influences. His Puritanism was not yet in conflict
with his classicism, his episcopalianism, or his royalism. Mr.
Tillyard,[12] on the basis of a letter to Alexander Gill, dated
May 1628, contends that Milton was in favor of the Petition
of Rights against Charles. Certainly by the time Milton came
to write *Lycidas* (1637) he was fully aware of the corruption
of the clergy and was ready to denounce the bishops—

> Blind mouths! that scarce themselves know how to hold
> A Sheep-hook.[13]

It is interesting to note that entries made in the *Commonplace
Book* in this same year indicate that Milton's suspicion of the
clergy was accompanied by a suspicion of the monarchy. Han-

[10] E. K. Rand, "Milton in Rustication," *SP,* XIX (1922), pp. 109–135.
[11] Cf. Tillyard, p. 22. Hatred of Roman Catholicism was a stronger
emotion in Milton at this stage than any feeling for or against the Stuarts.
James could be admired as a *Protestant* king.
[12] Tillyard, pp. 25–26.
[13] *Lycidas,* line 119.

ford, in commenting on this point, expresses surprise that the anti-royalist attitude should appear so soon:

> The setting down of the title "Census et Vectigal" is evidently connected with interest in the illegal exactions of Charles. And finally one note is definitely republican: "severus Sulpitius ait regium nomen semper liberis gentibus fere invisum." Were it not for the unquestionable evidence of the manuscript we should have been inclined, I think, to ascribe this last citation rather to the period of the *Tenure of Kings and Magistrates* (1649) than to that of *Lycidas* (1637). It will be remembered that in all the pamphlets written before the condemnation of King Charles in 1648-9 Milton carefully avoids saying or implying anything against the royal prerogative, and that in the *Second Defense* he takes pains to point out that he had not done so. That this was not for want of meditation on the subject or of what public policy required from him, we now see.[14]

But if we recognize that *Lycidas* is an "elegy on himself, on the churchman he had decided not to be," [15] the stock-taking of a young man who has left behind him the cloisters of Cambridge for an urgent practical world in which decisions for the future must be made and speedily made, it is not difficult to understand that a stand against the prelacy should have meant, at least privately, a stand against the king. The association of bishop and king in the famous phrase of James was an association in fact, and recognized as such by every Puritan reformer as well as by every royalist and every churchman. The Puritan element in Milton's thought might co-habit with classicism and Elizabethanism in the insulated student years; they might make common cause against the mediaevalism of Cambridge. Yet the first touch of the world was to force them apart. After 1637 a Latin poem in praise of King

---

[14] "Milton's Studies," *PMLA*, XXXVI (1921), pp. 297 ff.
[15] Haller, *The Rise of Puritanism*, p. 321.

James would have been an impossible task. And in *Paradise Regained* Milton was finally to attack classical humanism in its political aspects.

In other words, the cultural synthesis of Milton's student years could not be maintained outside the cloister. Milton left Cambridge and Horton to enter a torn and divided world of values, to take sides in a conflict which had been brewing since the last years of Elizabeth's reign and was now moving swiftly into the revolutionary phase. The loose synthesis of classical, Puritan, and Elizabethan elements had been illusory and epiphytic. Nevertheless, for a few brief but extremely important and impressionable years, Milton had felt something of the "first fine careless rapture" of the Elizabethans, and the direct untroubled inheritance he took from them he was not willingly to let die. This fact is decisive in explaining "the cultural lag" evident in Milton's poetry. Literary values and conventions still alive in books were to be contradicted by the death in fact of the world which had nourished them and given them meaning. New sensibilities were aroused in a society which had abandoned the compromise of Court and City for revolutionary struggle and eventual middle-class dictatorship. A new artistic centre of gravity had to be found, now that the unifying symbol of the crown was obsolete. As I have mentioned, there is some reason to believe that Milton took the side of Parliament against Charles as early as 1628. Although this does not necessarily imply a conversion to republicanism, it does suggest that kingship seemed already somewhat less than sacred. The *Commonplace Book* entry of 1637 (quoted by Hanford) shows that Milton was aware of the republican alternative to monarchy, and was giving it serious consideration, much earlier than might be expected. However, Milton was openly to defend the monarchy as late

as 1642 (with certain politic reservations), and was to keep
dead silence on the issue until 1649. Hilaire Belloc's suggestion
that this reticence was due merely to fear,[16] and Hanford's
more kindly conclusion that it was due to "public policy," [17]
fall short of the mark when one remembers not only Milton's
veneration for Cromwell (a king-worship of sorts), but also
the final document from his pen in praise of Sobieski, elected
king by the Polish people. "The implied contrast between the
courageous patriot Sobieski and the traitorous idler Charles II
was too sharp to be mistaken." [18] Charles is not "every inch
a king"—Sobieski is. The rule of the most worthy with full
consent of the sovereign people—this seems to be Milton's
final political position, and it is not very different from the
Elizabethan ideal. That ideal had died hard in Milton, and
it had died only because kingliness seemed no longer an attribute of kings. Milton's reluctance to abandon the Arthurian
legend as framework for his epic parallels his hesitancy to
make a public attack on the institution of kingship. The rejection of the monarchy may have been simple matter enough
for the pure politician or the pure fanatic, but Milton was
neither. For the poet such a rejection involved a way of thinking and feeling, a self-contained universe of associations and
sensibilities, the sense of continuity with the past. Consequently, it does not appear strange that Milton's poetry should
retain the royalist image and symbol well after Milton had
turned republican. But the poetic ideal and the political reality
were quite divorced, and his poetry suffered.

I have run ahead to problems beyond the scope of the
present chapter in order to suggest, for a moment, the per-

[16] *Milton,* Chap. III.
[17] "Milton's Studies," p. 298.
[18] Hanford, *A Milton Handbook,* p. 116.

sistence, or perhaps I should say the drag, of the Elizabethan ideal of kingship, a persistence, if you like, as an aesthetic habit rather than as an intellectual value. It is necessary at this point to discuss in some detail Milton's debt to Elizabethan literature. I have argued that Milton's closeness to the Elizabethans is due to a great extent to his early if temporary isolation from his own time, his momentary identification with Elizabethan enthusiasms, discoveries, and aspirations still heretical at Cambridge, and therefore still alive for the student.

The early poems show very clearly the fresh and immediate influence of Elizabethan literature. While still a boy at St. Paul's Milton learned from Alexander Gill not only a humanist reverence for the classics, but also a healthy respect for the writings of Englishmen, particularly Spenser, Sidney, Jonson and Campion.[19] That his reading of English literature was wider than the range of selection in Gill's *Logonomia Anglica* we can be sure, if only from the echoes in the poetry itself. *On the Death of a Fair Infant* is, as Tillyard has established, in the tradition of *Hero and Leander, Venus and Adonis,* and *The Passionate Pilgrim. In Quintem Novembris* indisputably shows a careful reading of Phineas Fletcher, and the conceits of the *Nativity Ode* are in the best manner of Giles Fletcher. Hanford regards this poem as in the direct line of succession of nativity odes by Jonson, Drummond, Beaumont, Southwell and Sylvester. "Finally, Milton's introduction of the personifications, Peace, Justice, Truth and Mercy, shows his familiarity with the allegory of the four daughters of God as developed by mediaeval writers and re-

---

[19] Tillyard, p. 10. I have drawn on Tillyard and on Hanford's *The Youth of Milton* and *A Milton Handbook* for much of the material on the Elizabethan antecedents of the early poems.

vived by Giles Fletcher in *Christ's Victory in Heaven*, whence Milton derived it." [20] *An Epitaph on the Marchioness of Winchester* is clearly in the tradition of Ben Jonson. Echoes of Burton, Beaumont and Fletcher sound unmistakably in *L'Allegro* and *Il Penseroso*. As Hanford has shown,[21] Milton, in writing *Comus*, drew for his plot on Peele's *Old Wives Tale*, and for episodes and situations on Fletcher's *The Faithful Shepherdess* and Ben Jonson's *Pleasure Reconciled*. For his allegory he is particularly indebted to Spenser,

> whose Bower of Bliss (*Faerie Queene*, Book II, Canto xii) is pre-sided over by the enchantress Acrasia, a Circe-like figure, the symbol of intemperance, and surrounded by creatures who have been transformed to beasts. That Milton had paid especial attention to the ethical meaning of this passage we know from *Areopagitica*.[22]

Indeed, the influence of Spenser is pervasive in the poem. Later, in the *Apology for Smectymnuus*, Milton was to acknowledge his youthful debt to Spenser:

> I betook me to those fables and romances, which recount in solemn cantos the deeds of knighthood founded by our victorious kings, and from hence in renown all over Christendom. There I read it in the oath of every knight that he should defend to the expense of his best blood, if so befell him the honor and chastity of virgin or matron; from whence even then I learned what a noble virtue chastity must be, to the defence of which so many worthies, by such a dear adventure of themselves, had sworn.[23]

Nothing could be clearer than this identification of Milton's early Puritanism with the courtly chivalric tradition of an Elizabethan poem alive enough and close enough to warm

---

[20] *Handbook*, p. 131.
[21] *Handbook*, pp. 146–150.
[22] *Handbook*, p. 147.
[23] *S.M.*, p. 549.

the moral sense of Milton without offending or even surprising his social or political sense. Milton does not hesitate to adapt royalist symbolism to his Puritan ethic.

There are reminiscences of Shakespeare, too, in such lines from *Comus* as:

> I know each lane, and every valley green. [310.]

> I was all eare,
> And took in strains that might create a soul
> Under the ribs of death. [560.]

> The pillar'd firmament is rott'ness
> And earth's base built on stubble. [597.]

It is interesting to note, however, that Milton's Puritanism led him to the courtly Spenser, paradoxically enough, rather than to Shakespeare, in whom bourgeois and courtly values are more subtly mingled. The poem *On Shakespeare,* with its debt to Jonson's "Thou art a monument without a tomb" and, probably, to William Browne's elegy on the Countess of Pembroke,[24] shows familiarity with Shakespeare and admiration for him, but implies as well that Shakespeare can never be a model. The "easy numbers," the "native woodnotes wild" of the spontaneous genius, happy though they be, belong to the periphery of art, inimitable and unprofitable. It is not enough to say here—"Neo-classicism!" One must stop to observe that Milton misses completely quite obvious elements in Shakespeare which he does *not* miss in Spenser. He selects Spenser's Arthur as the embodiment of virtue. He consciously adopts Spenser's royalist symbolism as the means of communicating positive moral values as well as nationalist and patriotic values. But he never so much as mentions the royalist heroes of Shakespeare, although there can

[24] *Handbook,* p. 133.

be no doubt that he was aware of them. He is attracted to the courtly Arthur and not to the soldier-citizen Henry V, Shakespeare's ideal king.

Certain clear-cut problems of interpretation have now emerged. It is evident, first of all, that Milton was immersed in Elizabethan poetry, and the freshness and zest of his early verse indicate that he was of the tradition, not outside attempting imitation. He does not seem conscious of any break with the Elizabethan world. Indeed, despite the rising hostility of Court and City, Milton as late as 1640 [25] regarded the royalist symbol as central in the presentation of values both patriotic and moral. In view of the letter to Gill in 1628, and the *Commonplace Book* entry of 1637, what is the significance for Milton's poetry of the divergence, already apparent, between the literary ideal and the political fact—between Arthur and Charles? Why was Milton drawn to Arthur rather than to the sturdy, popular ideal of kingship in Shakespeare? Was this a mere literary accident? Or was Milton's Elizabethanism limited by forces which can be defined, and does such limitation affect the early poems?

At first glance it might seem that Milton's absorption in Spenser was due entirely to the "sage and serious" morality of that "better teacher than Aquinas." There are indications, however, in Milton's use not only of the Arthurian material but also of other sources of national and patriotic legend that the *Faerie Queene* stood for something more than fine sermonizing. Note, for instance, the closing lines of *At a Vacation Exercise:*

> Rivers arise; whether thou be the Son,
> Of utmost *Tweed,* or *Oose,* or gulphie *Dun,*
> Of *Trent,* who like some earth-born Giant spreads

[25] *Epitaphium Damonis.*

His thirty Armes along the indented Meads,
Or sullen *Mole* that runneth underneath,
Or *Severn* swift, guilty of Maidens death,
Or Rockie *Avon,* or of Sedgie *Lee,*
Or Coaly *Tine,* or antient hallowed *Dee,*
Or *Humber* loud that keeps the *Scythians* Name,
Or *Medway* smooth, or Royal Towred *Thame.*[26]

Tillyard's comment on this passage is illuminating:

These smooth-running couplets dealing with English geography derive immediately from Browne's *Britannia's Pastorals,* whose first two parts were published in 1613 and 1616, the second part, therefore, but twelve years before Milton's poem. *But the references to early British mythology* [27] *suggest that Milton, like Browne's seniors, Spenser and Drayton, connected a geographical scene with a complete framework of Tudor patriotism.* The cumulative force of the reference is undoubted. The maiden of whose death the Severn was guilty is Sabrina, daughter of Locrine, himself son of Brutus, founder of the British nation; while the previous reference to the earth-born giant suggests the inhabitants found by Brutus and Corineus in Albion. The Dee is "hallowed" because frequented by the Druids . . . Finally the Thames is called "Royal Towred" not only to recall Windsor and Hampton but also, probably, to connect the royal lines of Tudor and Stuart with the early British Kings.[28]

Perhaps the best known "geographical epic" of the Elizabethan age is Drayton's *Polyolbion.* Similar in little to Drayton's method is the procession of rivers in *Faerie Queen,* IV, ii. As Lewis Ball has shown,[29] the patriotic epic, often associating place names with events and people typical of England's

[26] Lines 91–100.
[27] References to English mythology occur also in *Lycidas, Arcades,* and *Comus.*
[28] In *Seventeenth Century Studies Presented to Sir Herbert Grierson,* pp. 214–215; italics mine.
[29] "The Background of the Minor English Renaissance Epics," *ELH,* I, pp. 63–89.

glory, is a creation of Tudor times, reflecting the rise of England to national greatness. It is a literary phenomenon as expressive of the period as Shakespeare's chronicle plays. And here is Milton in the year 1628, the year of the letter to Gill, writing not only like a Tudor patriot, but even a Stuart patriot, if Tillyard's interpretation of "Royal Towred Thame" can be accepted. At least it is certain that Milton is associating the monarchy, whether Tudor or Stuart, with early British legend, and with patriotic suggestion.

Milton's intense nationalism of the Tudor pattern, clearly associated with royalist and courtly values, runs through the early poems, both Latin and English. The allusion to the "throngs of Knights and Barons bold" in *L'Allegro,* the repetition of the Sabrina motif in *Comus,* the direct statement of his intention to write an Arthurian epic in *Mansus* and *Epitaphium Damonis,* indicate that Milton is not only a "late Elizabethan" in his desire to glorify England, but also in the means chosen, namely, the identification of the "victorious king" with victorious England.

It must be borne in mind that the significance of the Arthurian legend was more literary than arbitrary.[30] The Tudor line had claimed to be descended from the Welsh Arthur, and the Arthurian reference was an important part of the chivalric cult revived at the court of Elizabeth. The sense of a romantic past fused emotively with the sense of a triumphant present had gone into the royalist symbol, creating for the Elizabethan a complex literary value in which "each kind Does straight its own resemblance find." The merchant, the

---

[30] For the Arthurian material I am indebted to Tillyard, to Miss Brinkley's *Arthurian Legend in the Seventeenth Century,* and to Greenlaw's *Studies in Spenser's Historical Allegory.*

apprentice, the gentleman, and the noble of the court could each see something of himself reflected in that symbol.

James had sought to keep alive the Arthurian association, as did Charles I. No poet writing in 1640 could be unaware of the connection between the traditional Arthurian story and the pretensions of the Stuarts. That Milton soon became uncomfortable about the connotation of the Arthurian legend in a world pregnant with revolutionary change is clear in the *Reason of Church Government,* written in 1642. In stating his determination to write a great English poem, he makes a remark about his choice of hero which shows that he is fully conscious of the new political difficulties confronting the poetic tradition as derived from the Elizabethans:

Time serves not now, and perhaps I might seem too profuse to give any certain account of what the mind at home, in the spacious circuits of her musing, hath liberty to propose to herself, though of highest hope and hardest attempting; whether that epic form whereof the two poems of Homer, and those other two of Virgil and Tasso, are a diffuse, and the book of Job a brief model: or whether the rules of Aristotle herein are strictly to be kept, or nature to be followed, which in them that know art, and use judgment, is no transgression, but an enriching of art: and lastly, what king or knight, *before the conquest,* might be chosen in whom to lay the pattern of a Christian hero.[31]

Note the uncertainty. The avowed resolution in *Epitaphium Damonis* to write an Arthurian epic is now reduced to a question. However, the hero who will embody the Christian virtues in a poem "doctrinal to a nation" will still be a "king or knight." The literary tradition of Spenser, reinforced by Tasso and Ariosto holds its appeal, though Milton, a few lines further on, considers the possibility of basing his epic

[31] *S.M.,* p. 525; italics mine.

on the Greek or the Hebraic mythology. But he is uncomfortable. This comes out most clearly in the passage above, specifying a king or knight "before the conquest." The phrase betrays not only Milton's Parliamentarian sympathies, but implies also a rejection of the Arthurian legend. To quote Tillyard:

> Not long after Milton's birth, when James began offending Englishmen by claiming his divine right of kings, the more democratic scholars sought in Saxon law and custom a counterpoise to the royal claims. . . . It was this political motive that initiated the beginnings of Anglo-Saxon research in the early 17th century, and which tended to degrade the authority of Geoffrey of Monmouth, chief sponsor of early British myth. There was a growing tendency for British myth to be associated with the king and his supporters, and for Anglo-Saxon history to be associated with Parliament and its rights.[32]

A hero "before the conquest" is an Anglo-Saxon hero,[33] one in no way associated with the Stuart line, and one acceptable to the Parliamentary side. A king—and not a king. It is significant that among the notes for his proposed drama there is the following comment: "A heroical poem may be founded somewhere in Alfred's reign, especially at his issuing out of Edelingsey on the Danes; whose actions are well like those of Ulysses."[34] Surely there could be nothing amiss in an Anglo-Saxon king! But history was hurrying on the war and the scaffold. The royalist atom was split.

There can be little doubt, then, that Milton saw in King

---

[32] *Seventeenth Century Studies*, p. 219.

[33] The Parliamentarians and the "left" democrats regarded the Norman Conquest as the beginning of royalist tyranny. Winstanley's communism involves an appeal to pre-Norman law. As the Arthurian tradition had become attached to the Tudor and Stuart lines it was under attack as belonging culturally to post-Norman royalism.

[34] *S.M.*, p. 1131.

Arthur something more than a picturesque equation of a moral abstraction. The moral element was present. Milton's Puritanism need not be denied. But Spenserian nationalism, a feeling for the crown not only as the symbol of virtue and high conduct, but also as the symbol of triumphant nationhood, is present too. Milton, in planning an Arthurian epic, was not merely setting out to imitate a literary model in the interest of morality. He was seeking to participate in a great tradition which remained alive for him and in him after it had died. Milton's rejection of Arthur was simply Milton's awakening to a condition of division and struggle which had existed in the real world since Milton's birth but which had not been visible from the happy island of study and youthful aspiration.

The dismissal of Arthur clearly implies a dissociation, a breaking apart of values. The poet with Parliamentarian sympathies, no matter how great his reverence for English tradition and the reign of Elizabeth, could no longer express his reverence in the royalist terms appropriate to the tradition. The crown was now a symbol of disunity, not unity. That Milton should consider Alfred as a kind of well-fumigated Arthur indicates merely the tenacity of a literary habit. Certainly to deprive the epic hero not only of Stuart but also of Elizabethan associations would be to leave him a mere skeleton without the flesh of suggestion for either citizen or courtier. Nevertheless, the fact that Milton does consider Alfred as a possible hero is significant. The Spenserian habit is so much a part of his literary equipment that on the very edge of revolution he still consciously looks for a royalist hero who can be a central epic figure without offending the political sensibilities of the Parliamentarian. Such a figure, though inoffensive, would be wholly negative, and could not be made to carry the suggestion of English greatness *after* the conquest. Milton was to abandon the royalist epic. In my next chapter, on *Paradise Lost,* I shall have something to say about his ultimate choice of a biblical subject. But it must be stressed here that Milton's reluctance to discard the Arthurian project and the Elizabethan identification of king and triumphant nationhood derived from Spenser, demonstrates not only the hold of the Spenserian ideal on Milton's conscious thinking, but also helps one to understand why Milton, well after a rejection of the kingly hero was forced upon him by political events, should continue in *Paradise Lost,* perhaps unconsciously, to make use of royalist allusion and reference in a sense often contradictory to his ostensible purpose. Milton did not admit a break with the Elizabethan tradition until 1649. And after the idol was shattered the fragments still appeared. The dilemma of *Paradise Lost,* the conflict of royalist imagery and anti-royalist ideology, derives from this belated Elizabethan apprenticeship of Milton's, this temporary illusion of a present past. It is not enough, then, to say with Tillyard that Milton drops the Arthurian legend because of now unfortunate royalist associations. One must also recognize that the unfortunate, because sometimes inappropriate, royalism of *Paradise Lost* is because of Milton's long absorption in the Arthurian theme and all it suggested to the Elizabethan sensibility. The early poems and the early plans, seen properly against the Elizabethan setting as well as against the lengthening shadow of the English Revolution, illustrate the crisis of poetry in a changing world. Far from being "outside" or "above" his age, Milton is in the very centre of it, "between two worlds, one dead, the other powerless to be born."

Note, for instance, the language and tone of the famous passage in *Of Reformation* in which Milton hints that his great poem may have for its hero not Arthur but the leaders of Parliament:

> Then, amidst the hymns and hallelujahs of saints, some one may perhaps be heard offering at high strains in new and lofty measures to sing and celebrate thy divine mercies and marvellous judgments in this land throughout the ages; whereby this great and warlike nation, instructed and inured to the fervent and continual practice of truth and righteousness, and casting far from her the rags of her old vices, may press on hard to that high and happy emulation to be found the soberest, wisest, and most Christian people at that day, when, thou, the eternal and shortly expected king, shalt open the clouds to judge the several kingdoms of the world, and distributing national honors and rewards to religious and just commonwealths, shalt put an end to all earthly tyrannies, proclaiming thy universal and mild monarchy through heaven and earth; *where they undoubtedly, that by their labors, counsels and prayers, have been earnest for the common good of religion and their country, shall receive above the inferior orders of the blessed, the regal addition of principalities, legions, and thrones into their glorious titles.*[35]

Milton's nationalism is unabated, though the rags of old vices, Episcopacy, the divine right of kings (and so Arthur), must be thrown aside and "the mild monarchy" of Christ welcomed. But Milton will have a Parliamentarian Arthur—he will make Brutus king!

The leaders of Parliament will take crowns and thrones, will become regal saints, glittering above their inferiors like a multiple Arthur, regenerate and mighty. Soon Milton would discard these "new Presbyters" for Cromwell, the collective Arthur for the single. In *Paradise Lost,* as I shall show, the leader with the virtue, the strength, and the gentility of Arthur, alone is "regenerate." In the Polish *Manifesto,* Sobieski seems to be the final substitute for the Arthurian ideal.

[35] *S.M.,* p. 469; italics mine.

During the actual years of the revolution and after, then, the "king-obsession" as derived from Spenser comes out indirectly and perhaps unconsciously in scattered and usually inappropriate royalist metaphor and simile, and directly in the presentation of the aristocratic ideal, the sainted regenerate gentleman, discreetly shorn of his crown and his literary antecedents but never of his class position above "the rabble."

Hilaire Belloc (oddly enough) has pointed out [36] more clearly than anyone else that Milton's inflexible aristocratic outlook was in no small measure due to the peculiar isolation and security of his boyhood and young manhood. Not only did he have the protected leisure in which to acquaint himself with the master spirits of the past; he had the social opportunity to meet the master spirits of the present—from Manso to the Countess Dowager of Derby. His undemocratic contempt for the masses may find suitable rationalization in Puritan doctrines of salvation—but there were many doctrines to choose from, some of which granted salvation rather lavishly to those unfortunates outside the gleaming ranks of the elect.[37] One might assume that the distinction which Milton made between the regenerate and the unregenerate was a theological approximation to the distinction in the real world between the upper-middle-class Parliamentarians and those troublesome elements to the "left of centre." Indeed, Milton's first identification with the revolutionary cause was in alliance with the Presbyterians, "the middle sort of men," ranged as a class against the monarchy. This was class war, and Milton knew it. But he was drawn to it because it seemed to be fundamentally a war between the real aristocrat and the nominal aristocrat, between St. Paul and Laud, between

[36] Chap. I.
[37] See Woodhouse, *Puritanism and Liberty,* Introduction.

Arthur and Charles. At first Parliament seemed the new aristocracy of the spirit, the occupants of a philosophical realm which Charles and his court had abdicated—and Milton attached to the Parliamentarians the deserted symbolism of royalty. And it would seem like straightforward characteristic Puritanism to cast out of this blessed realm all those who through natural inferiority, indifference, or misguided sentiment for Charles nominated themselves for damnation. But Milton was to find more and more candidates for damnation—the Parliamentarians themselves, and finally even Cromwell. While it is true, then, that Milton participated in the first stages of the struggle as a conscious middle-class revolutionary (and clearly because he fancied that he saw a resemblance between his own aristocratic idealism and the Calvinist principles of the Parliamentarians), it is equally true that Milton moved further and further away from the merchants, whom he damns, and the "rabble," whom he scorns.

In discussing the aristocratic element in Milton's thought Professor Woodhouse has this to say:

Wherever the clear-cut Puritan distinction between the regenerate and the unregenerate operates strongly, as it does in Milton's thought, one may get an unlimited emphasis on individual liberty, and may even find this liberty demanded for all; but one will not get fundamental democracy, for democracy means the addition of equality to liberty. To ground the claim for liberty on the idea of Christian liberty is to assume a distinction between Christians and other men and to build into your conception of liberty itself the idea of basic inequality, the inequality between the regenerate and the unregenerate. *In so doing Milton illustrates in an extreme degree what may be called the "aristocratic" element inherent in the Puritan position.*[38]

[38] "Milton, Puritanism, and Liberty," *University of Toronto Quarterly,* Vol. IV, no. 4 (July, 1935), pp. 496–497; italics mine.

This aristocratic outlook strongly affected Milton's practical politics. He moved step by step "to the right" until, in *A Ready and Easy Way to Establish a Free Commonwealth,* he came out for government by an *actual* blue-blooded aristocracy, apparently the nearest approximation to that "aristocracy of the spirit" to be found after all. He still roars against the nominal king and the English monarchical tradition, but surely the following passage could not be written by a man who held a detached theological conception of aristocracy:

> The other part of our freedom consists in the civil rights and advancements of every person according to his merit; the enjoyment of those never more certain, and the access to these never more open, than in a free commonwealth. Both which, in my opinion, may be best and soonest obtained, if every county in the land were made a kind of subordinate commonalty or common-' wealth, and one chief town or more, according as the shire is in circuit, made cities, if they be not so called already; *where the nobility and the chief gentry, from a proportionate compass of territory annexed to each city, may build houses or palaces befitting their quality; may bear part in the government, make their own judicial laws, or use those that are, and execute them by their own elected judicature and judges without appeal, in all things of civil government between man and man. So they shall have justice in their own hands, law executed fully and finally in their own counties, long wished and spoken of, but never yet obtained.*[39]

It is true that this pamphlet was written in desperation and despair. Milton had already ceased hoping for a nation both virtuous and mighty led by a minority, but a sufficient minority, of self-certified saints, of true-blue Arthurs. The next best thing apparently was the rule of actual if not ideal nobles and gentry, "with justice in the hands" of the Sir Artegalls of the shires, who might "judge without appeal."

[39] *S.M.,* p. 912; italics mine.

This is not unlike Plato's retreat from the ideal aristocracy of *The Republic* to the less than lovely, but eminently practical, realism of *The Laws*. But *The Laws* and the *Ready and Easy Way* express more than weariness, more than resignation. They are tired and final revelations of a class position inherent in the earlier idealism.[40] Unfortunately for the purity and consistency of Milton's thought, and therefore of the poetic expression of it, the "type" of perfection which he wanted in the state and in the individual could not be found in the court, the episcopacy, or the person of Charles. Spenser's Arthur, the "type" of virtue, poise, and power, is for his age and class at once the first gentleman of the spirit and the first gentleman of the land. And the Arthurian ideal, essentially Platonic, was given substance by a possible identification with a real aristocracy. For Spenser and contemporary. poets of his class, there was some apparent and satisfying approximation of fact and ideal. And just here the difference between Spenser and Shakespeare must be noted. Spenser's

[40] I do not wish to seem unfair to Milton's politics. His role in the revolutionary period taken by and large was a progressive role. When one looks at him against a writer like Dryden his reputation as a libertarian is safe by comparison. He was not a democrat—nor was Cromwell. But in the period before the fall of the Commonwealth seemed certain—before the *Ready and Easy Way*—Milton *in effect* if not by intention, gave expression to the advanced interests of the middle class. These interests were *ultimately* in the direction of democracy, though temporarily at least they confounded the democratic aspirations of the majority in England. Objectively, in historical perspective, Milton's early political writing is progressive. My problem, however, is more complex than that of the political historian: the artistic process must reflect Milton's *subjective* view of his world. Milton's class psychology is a tug-of-war between the objective middle-class movement to which he had allied himself, and the aristocratic cultural tradition to which he seemed bound by artistic and philosophical inclination. One cannot but feel that in Milton the cultural tradition triumphed over the political affiliation. Philosophically and artistically Milton tried to *understand* the bourgeois revolution in aristocratic terms. My treatment of this phenomenon is meant not as a condemnation but as an explanation.

king is half Platonic, a fashioning of the "type" of virtue, and half courtier, a reflection of a reality particularized in the flesh and blood of men like Sidney and Raleigh. But Shakespeare's king is a compound of Sidney and Simon Eyre, of the courtier and the citizen. Even to his little finger he is without abstraction. He is not fashioned after an ideal concept. He takes his life, and derives his democratic dignity, from that happy mingling of class interests which I described in the first chapter. The aristocrat of a later generation (Milton, or the neo-classic critic of the eighteenth century) might well see in Henry V vulgarity rather than dignity. Milton avoids the Shakespearian king, and the neo-classicists draw upon the more purely aristocratic models of Latin and Greek literature. This "shift in sensibility" is *not* accidental. It represents the narrowing of a class outlook, the sharpening of a social focus. Class antagonisms, discernible by the close of Elizabeth's reign, ripened into conflict in the Civil Wars, and sulked through the Restoration into the separate codes of social discrimination which characterized creative work and criticism in the first half of the eighteenth century. The aristocratic code of the "honnête homme" clashed with the sentimental code of the bourgeois "man of feeling." The sensibility of the age was divided. Shakespeare represents clearly a unified sensibility. Even in Spenser, because of the common national feeling for the crown, and because, too, of a partial but subtle penetration of bourgeois values into the psychology of the courtier, there is some reflection of the class compromise which underlined Elizabethan culture at its height. But in Spenser the bourgeois element is in disguise, informing the motivation but not the appearance of his art, whereas in Shakespeare, as I have shown, it is direct and obvious, getting into the very speech and actions of his kingly hero.

Milton was attracted to Spenser not only because his early "intellectual milieu" was the Renaissance and was unaffected by the disintegrating forces of the early seventeenth century, but also because his study of Plato's idealism and the Puritan doctrine of the Elect gave ideological form to a self-esteem nourished from the cradle by awe-stricken parents, parents who protected him from the contamination of the world, set him among his peers at Cambridge, and later supported him in his role of philosopher-king at Horton. Professor Haller says: "We are not told in Milton's spiritual autobiography the precise moment when he felt the conviction of grace. The sense of personal election seems to have been his from the start." [41] Certainly he undergoes none of the orgies of self-reproach attendant upon the conversion of religious men of feeling in the period. Milton's Puritanism is intellectual, it is Platonic, and it is aristocratic. In the early poems Platonic and Spenserian elements are closely intermingled. As I have pointed out, following Tillyard, epic suggestions in *L'Allegro* and *Il Penseroso*, of "Knights and Barons Bold," of "Turneys and of Trophies hung" are entirely within the Arthurian tradition. At the same time, evidently, Milton is deep in Plato:

> Or let my lamp at midnight hour,
> Be seen in som high lonely Towr,
> Where I may oft out-watch the *Bear*,
> With thrice great *Hermes*, or unsphear
> The spirit of Plato to unfold
> What Worlds, or what vast regions hold
> The immortal mind that hath forsook
> Her mansion in this fleshy nook.[42]

What is more suggestive is the juxtaposition of Plato and Spenser in *Comus*. I have already noted Milton's indebtedness

[41] *The Rise of Puritanism*, p. 320.
[42] *Il Penseroso*, lines 85–92.

to Spenser in this poem. The conception here of virtue, of
chastity, despite Puritan-Christian overtones, is essentially
Platonic:

> So dear to Heav'n is Saintly chastity,
> That when a soul is found sincerely so,
> A thousand liveried Angels lacky her,
> Driving far off each thing of sin and guilt,
> And in cleer dream, and solemn vision
> Tell her of things that no gross ear can hear,
> Till oft convers with heav'nly habitants
> Begin to cast a beam on th' outward shape,
> The unpolluted temple of the mind,
> And turn it by degrees to the souls essence,
> Till all be made immortal: but when lust
> By unchaste looks, loose gestures, and foul talk,
> But most by leud and lavish act of sin,
> Lets in defilement to the inward parts,
> The soul grows clotted by contagion,
> Imbodies, and imbrutes, till she quite loose
> The divine property of her first being.[43]

The Lady of *Comus* is of the Elect. The "liveried Angels" secure her predestined salvation. But the concept of virtue as a
"type" of eternity capable of transforming the physical body
itself to the "soul's essence" goes beyond Calvinism to the
reaches of Platonic thought. At this point the aristocratic
aspects of Puritanism and Platonism meet, as they do in
Spenser's idea of the virtuous Arthur. As Professor Woodhouse points out,[44] the identification of virtue with inner liberty transcends Puritanism and puts Milton in the company
of the Cambridge Platonists. "Love virtue, she alone is free."
And Milton was to follow the will-o'-the-wisp ideal from
Arthur, to the Parliamentarians, to Cromwell, to the blue-
bloods of the parishes, to Sobieski. He sought in the real for

[43] Lines 453–469.
[44] "Milton, Puritanism, and Liberty," pp. 498–499.

some reflection of the ideal, the aristocratic "type." It is for this reason, perhaps, that he is one of the most "literary" of poets. New symbols of power and worth proper to the contemporary aspirations and deeds of Parliament, of the middle class, of Cromwell, and of the Independents, do not emerge from life into the poetry of Milton. He is not looking at the affairs of his time; he is looking *through* them. He is trying to solve an equation in which the real and the ideal are involved—an equation which will not come out right. When an element in the equation seems useful, he seizes upon it with the instinct of the mathematician. For instance, in the stage of the revolution when an appeal to popular rights constituted an effective weapon against the corruption and tyranny of the church and the monarchy, Milton extols "the people." [45] The meanest citizen is capable of participating in church government. The "plain artisan" who is "solid" and "conscientious" is, indeed, the backbone of the nation. In *Areopagitica* he argued that "the people had the capacity for following a true leader to the heights of freedom." (Note the "true leader," the republican Arthur! Nevertheless the people are regarded as capable of recognizing virtue in the leader and are considered indispensable in achieving the New Jerusalem.) In *The Tenure of Kings and Magistrates* he proclaims the people's right to revolt, and seems close to Lilburne's position. But once it is clear that the majority of the people are not in support of the regicide, Milton in *Eikonoklastes* writes a bitter tirade against the masses, and turns once more to the thin red line of God's aristocrats. That abstract concept "the people" has been discarded as useless in solving

---

[45] In *Apology for Smectymnuus*. See Wolfe, "Milton, Lilburne, and the People," *MP*, XXXI (1934), pp. 253–272, for a discussion of early democratic tendencies.

the equation. My point is not that Milton's anger was not natural or even justified, but rather that the attack was more in anger than in sorrow, that "the people" was an abstraction of no more regard than if the figure 2 had provokingly upset his calculations. This same cold anger characterizes his ultimate dismissal of "the middle sort of men," as corrupt and selfish now as the "Blind Mouths" in *Lycidas*.

The preoccupation with an ideal, a "type" of virtue, limited Milton's poetic perception. Not only did it keep him to the symbolism of the past, causing him to reward Parliamentarians with crowns; it likewise prevented him from mining new poetic ore in the political and social life of his time. Like Spenser he absorbed certain bourgeois values, as witness the domestic quality of his love-poetry. But although his attitudes were affected by the "intellectual climate" of the citizen's England, his fundamental ideals remained aristocratic, tying him to the courtly, even royalist tradition of English poetry—the royalist tradition of Spenser, not Shakespeare. Milton's Elizabethanism *was* limited. Not only does Shakespeare's royalist hero fail to attract him; Milton is incapable of understanding, and therefore of imitating, the poetic process which drew the portrait of Henry V not from an ideal vision, but from the unity-in-complexity of Elizabethan life, of Elizabethan class characteristics. It is true that the Elizabethan compromise was over by Milton's time, but as I have shown, Milton during his student years seemed quite unaware of the change which had come over his world. If the future secretary to Cromwell, the one-day champion of Christian liberty, had turned to the popular bourgeois kings of Shakespeare and equated them with the glory of England, how different a poet and how different a political theorist we might have had. But, of course, the very circumstances which projected Milton's youthful mind into the Elizabethan world, saw to it that he went as an aristocrat, even a snob, and quite unprepared to understand, or, for that matter, observe the impact of class values on literature and life. Indeed, if Milton had realized the class implications of his day, he would have been debarred from Elizabethanism, would have seen it as a dead glory, as John Donne finally saw it.

Before approaching *Paradise Lost,* a poem written for "fit audience though few," for the aristocrats of the spirit by an aristocrat of the spirit, it is essential to recognize clearly this paradox of the Puritan Royalist, of the belated Elizabethan in search of the lost Spenserian ideal—searching for the pearl of great price sometimes in the gutter, and even willing at times to call the gutter blessed. For it is in *Paradise Lost, Paradise Regained,* and *Samson Agonistes* that Milton's dilemma is most apparent. Many of his early poems are play pieces, often alive with Elizabethan lyricism, but casual and occasional and scarcely indicative of Milton's main interests. I have already shown the bearing of the more important of these poems on the central problem under discussion. The aristocratic nationalism and royalism of the early work is obvious enough. However, because of the contrast it affords with the royalism of *Paradise Lost,* I have left to the end of this chapter a discussion of the quality of some of the more significant royalist allusions and images in the early poems. And I will attempt at this point to answer the question which I raised earlier in this chapter: In view of the letter to Gill in 1628, and the *Commonplace Book* entry of 1637, what is the significance for Milton's early poetry of the divergence, already apparent, between the literary ideal and the political fact—between Arthur and Charles?

As one might expect, Milton's early poems in the Eliza-

bethan tradition are studded with conventional royalist allusions. Christ, "a sov'ran priest," stoops his "regal head." . . .[46]
"Kings for such a tomb should want to die. . . .[47] A lad who
is outstanding among his fellows, "O're all his brothers he
shall Reign as King." . . .[48] The magic root of *Comus* is treas-
ured "as of sov'ran use." . . .[49] Shrines are "princely," [50] gods
are "enthron'd," [51] the Lady of *Arcades* is a "rural Queen." [52]
Such a list could be prolonged indefinitely. The complimentary use of the royalist allusion is, of course, the stock-in-trade
of Elizabethan poetry, and Milton adopts it without question. Such phrases were part of a poetic diction which had
originated in a genuine enough admiration for kingship.
True, to call a head "regal" was not necessarily to profess
monarchical politics. A Daughter of the American Revolution may without a twinge call a pumpkin pie "fit for a king"
to this day! Taken by itself, the simple complimentary reference to an attribute of royalty carries no great significance.
However, the repeated use of such allusions by an aristo-
cratically minded youth immersed in Elizabethan literature
and contemplating an Arthurian epic of his own *is* a matter
of some significance. One is forced to note that the royalist
allusion is not applied to old Hobson, the University Carrier,
a prosperous "little merchant" of the town. Everyman is not
a king in these Hobson "elegies" in which humour and affection and gentlemanly condescension mingle. Christ and
Moloch may both be kings—but Hobson never. Later, the

[46] *The Passion,* line 15.
[47] *On Shakespeare,* line 16.
[48] *At a Vacation Exercise,* line 75.
[49] *Comus,* line 638.
[50] *Arcades,* line 36.
[51] *Comus,* line 10.
[52] Line 94.

leaders of Parliament are kings for a day—their followers not for an instant. Milton's aristocratic sense knew whom to crown, and whom not to crown.

The allusions to which I have referred thus far, typical of what I have called the "complimentary" use of royalism, carry the suggestion of rank, of leadership. They are aristocratic signposts definite enough as to the direction in which they point, but fleshless, unparticularized, tending even to the cliché. Astoreth is "Queen" of Heaven,[53] Moloch is a "grisly king." [54] The sense of value as distinguished from the sense of rank is attached to rather than included in the royalist allusion. Moloch is a "king"—but "grisly." Astoreth's dubious queenliness comes out through a complex set of associations with pagan evil. In other words, royalism is used in the early poems to provide aristocratic but abstract suggestions of rank rather than warm and inclusive suggestions of quality.

The *Nativity Ode* reveals a clear contrast between "the mild monarchy of Christ" and the real monarchies of the world. "Heaven's eternal King" is not John Donne's sublimated Stuart but

> That glorious *Form*, that *Light* unsufferable,
> And that far-beaming *blaze of Majesty*.[55]

The "Prince of Light" [56] resides not in a bigger and better Whitehall but in "the Courts of Everlasting Day." [57] The Kings of earth [58] with their useless spears and shields and chariots and trumpets are immobilized by the coming of the ideal king, the pure Platonic "Form" of monarchy, at once

[53] *Nativity Ode,* line 201.
[54] Line 209.
[55] Line 8.
[56] Line 62.
[57] Line 13.
[58] Stanza IV (The Hymn).

first in rank and first in spirit, but naked of all earthly royalist associations. Here we are reminded of the Cambridge Platonists who would describe God only in terms of light and pure form. Milton differs from them in keeping the suggestion of rank, the aristocratic ideal, but he is far from associating Christ's kingship with the kingship of England as were the Platonists themselves. There are occasional lapses into earthly symbolism in the description of heaven which, in stanza XV, is a "high Palace Hall" with gates. "The helmed Cherubim" and "sworded Seraphim" stand in "glittering ranks." [59] "The dreadfull Judge in middle Air shall spread his throne." [60] Milton's decorative sense occasionally seems in conflict with his idealist conception. But, as Arthur Barker has convincingly demonstrated, the fundamental symbolism of the poem turns on the twin ideas of light and musical harmony. The kingdom of "The Prince of Light" is idealist, a universal principle of order and harmony:

> Christ is the reason for the angelic music and the source of the music of the spheres, which, at his birth, should harmonize with the choir and produce in men the harmony of their first perfection. [61]

The musical symbol of order reappears again and again in the early poems, notably in *Il Penseroso, The Passion, Upon the Circumcision, At a Solemn Music, Arcades, Comus,* and *Ad Patrem.* It is derived apparently from his Cambridge reading of Plato and Aristotle,[62] and reflects his young Renaissance enthusiasm for the ideas and forms of classical thought

[59] Stanza XI.
[60] Line 84.
[61] "The Pattern of Milton's Nativity Ode," *U. of T. Quarterly,* Vol. X, No. 2 (Jan. 1941), p. 177.
[62] Barker, p. 178.

in those happy days when he was at once a classicist, a Puritan, and a Spenserian.

The conclusion is inevitable that the royalist allusions in Milton's early poems come from the traditions of the past rather than from the reality of the present. The complimentary allusions reflecting Milton's aristocratic deference to rank and title do not conflict with the social hierarchy of the day. But neither is it nourished by that hierarchy, remaining abstract and fleshless. As I have shown, specific qualities must be attached to the symbol if it is to carry more than the suggestion of rank. And when Milton describes the monarchy of Christ he labors to avoid any confusion with the monarchy of earth. It may be objected here that Milton's "Prince of Light" is patterned after the Scriptures and therefore could not conceivably carry royalist suggestions of a contemporary coloring. But Donne was as deep in the Scriptures as Milton, yet for a while he saw a family resemblance between the King of Heaven and the King of England. The whole evidence of Milton's reading in Elizabethan literature, his early enthusiasm for Spenser and the Arthurian ideal, and his aristocratic outlook, tend to prove that he was not unaware of all the connotations of "Prince." But he attaches to the title a quality which has not, nor was meant to have, contemporary reference. Note that again, in the *Epitaph on the Marchioness of Winchester*,[63] when he wants to give to the title "Queen" a celestial quality transcending earthly rank, he does it with the "blazing Majesty and Light" of Heaven. The Marchioness becomes a Queen—but a Queen of Heaven, a Queen with a difference. The Court of Heaven is no longer described in the image of the English Court, nor is the English Court a prototype of Heaven. The ideal is quite detached from the real.

[63] Line 70.

In 1637 Milton wrote a distinctly republican comment into his *Commonplace Book,* and he wrote *Lycidas* with its bitter rejection of the Episcopacy. Yet, in the vein of the *Nativity Ode,* Lycidas ascends to Heaven:

> So *Lycidas* sunk low, but mounted high,
> Through the dear might of him that walk'd the waves
> Where other groves, and other streams along,
> With *Nectar* pure his oozy Lock's he laves
> And hears the unexpressive nuptiall Song,
> In the blest Kingdoms meek of joy and love.
> There entertain him all the Saints above,
> In solemn troops, and sweet Societies
> That sing, and singing in their glory move.[64]

The Kingdom of Heaven is a Kingdom but "meek" (unlike the English Church) and compact of "joy and love" qualitatively manifested by the symbol of music. Divinity here doth hedge a kingdom out of all verisimilitude.

But the kingly ideal, the royal "type," remains in Milton's religious references as it remained in his plans for the epic well after the last moment in which he might possibly have had respect for the Stuarts. The almost perfunctory nature of the "complimentary" royalist allusions, taken into account with the idealist nature of his religious and epic royalism, indicates that Milton derived his values from a sense of the past, from Plato, from Spenser, from the Christian tradition—never from Charles.

With the somewhat doubtful exception of his "Royal Towred *Thame*" in the *Vacation Exercise* the only reference to the Stuarts in his early poems is contained in the group celebrating Guy Fawkes Day. Milton was seventeen when he wrote *In Quintem Novembris,* and as I have pointed out, it is little more than an experiment in the classical epic. Milton

[64] Lines 172–180.

was attracted to the subject perhaps because of his anti-Catholic bias, perhaps because the machinery for the epic had been provided by Fletcher. At any rate, here was the opportunity to write on a national subject in the classical tradition, and Milton wrote with the classical and Elizabethan conventions well in hand. "Good King James," the epic hero of the best tradition, sits on his throne, "without thought of hidden conspiracy or open enemy." [65] This is stretching the truth, but Milton is working out a dramatic opposition in which the naïve goodness of England's King is contrasted with the scheming malice of the Triple Tyrant, the tool of Satan. God intervenes in the nick of time; England, personified by King and nobles, is saved from the Gunpowder Plot; and Satanic Catholicism is dealt a final and crushing defeat.

Only in this short Latin epic and in the four short epigrams on the Gunpowder Plot does Milton identify a Stuart King with the fate of England or with the idea of "the good." *In Quintem Novembris* was written in 1626. In 1629 he wrote the letter to Gill with its hint of Parliamentarian sympathies. Certainly it is significant that although Milton was to ponder the Arthurian epic and to stud his early poems with royalist allusion, he never again made a direct reference to Stuart royalism or even, in the kind of allusion, implied a reference to the contemporary line which had in it anything more than a suggestion of rank.

There is an untroubled and uncontaminated purity about the early poetic royalism which suggests absorption in a vision of the ideal "type." It is when Milton seeks to realize the ideal in the political actual that his poetic idiom becomes confused. In *Paradise Lost* the clear distinction between the ideal and the real breaks down, and there is war in Heaven.

[65] For English translation see *S.M.*, pp. 96 ff.

Just as Milton's ideal aristocrat finally takes on a guise all too human, so Milton's ideal king takes on the likeness of the despot. With the shock of the Revolution, the struggle for real power intrudes. And the concept of king assumes less visionary attributes.

III

Paradise Lost

BEFORE analyzing the significance of royalist symbolism in *Paradise Lost,* it will be necessary to place this poem in the context of Milton's thought, and in the context of history itself. I have shown that in the early poems royalism, when it carries more than an aristocratic suggestion of rank, is used by Milton to convey an abstract ideal quite dissociated from any contemporary reference. Both Arthur and the "Prince of Light" are Platonic rather than Caroline. The kingship of God and Christ, the order and control of the universe, is expressed by symbols of light after the fashion of the Cambridge Platonists, or in terms of music and mathematics. The early poetic work suggests not so much hostility to the Stuarts as comparative indifference, owing to a preoccupation with ideals which, it so happened, had been brought to Milton in a literary tradition of royalist dress. The Spenserian royalist idiom of the poetry before *Paradise Lost* is not inappropriate to an aristocratic spirit creating in what was almost a political vacuum. In those relatively untroubled years before the storm, Platonic-Spenserian values and aristocratic deference to earthly rank are held in separate suspension within the royalist symbol. There is no confusion. God is not colored with Caesar, nor Caesar with God.

In *Paradise Lost* God is Caesar. The order of the universe is no longer a mathematical harmony drenched in light, but a mighty tyranny. Heaven is now a glittering barbaric court of warriors, of feudal princes and barons. The dominating symbol of Milton's new Heaven is not light but *power*. God is the utter and absolute despot ruling by decree, crushing revolt and dissension by military force. And this is the poem of a man ostensibly a republican who had abandoned the royalist Arthuriad. This is the poem of the man who had once written:

> The kings of this world have both ever hated and instinctively feared the church of God; whether it be for that their doctrine seems much to favor two things to them so dreadful, liberty and equality, or because they are the children of that kingdom which, as ancient prophecies have foretold, shall in the end break to pieces and dissolve all their great power and dominion.[1]

Why, one is forced to ask, is the kingdom which will one day "break to pieces" the illiberal kingdoms of the earth imagined as a despotism more autocratic and more "royal" than anything ever known to men? Why was Milton not content to oppose the monarchies of earth with the "mild monarchy" of Christ, a monarchy exemplifying those principles of Christian liberty for which he had striven? Clearly, the purpose behind this conception must be understood before single aspects of the style can be safely discussed.

The theme of *Paradise Lost* has been discussed by countless critics from Dr. Johnson to T. S. Eliot. The simple fact, of course, remains—Milton was attempting "to justify the ways of God to man." Scholars can give little credence to the "Satanic" school of interpretation. As E. N. S. Thompson [2] puts it, the central theme of the poem is "the origin and course of evil. . . . *Paradise Lost* shows how the right can and must prevail." Milton is not "of the devil's party." Fortunately for Milton criticism, debate on this point has died

---

[1] *Eikonoklastes* (*P.W.*, I, p. 434).
[2] "The Theme of *Paradise Lost*," *PMLA*, XXVIII (1913), p. 107.

away. The purpose of the poem in the broadest theological and ethical sense has been accepted pretty much as Milton wanted it accepted. But for the tribe of contemporary critics concerned with the political and social motivation of Milton's thought and art, complex problems involving "purpose" still remain. Granted that Milton consciously attempted "to justify the ways of God to man," was the attempt serene and confident, proceeding easily from basic and untroubled faith? Or was the justification a forced and anxious attempt to make the jagged ends of political and religious faith meet?

A recent article by Arnold Williams brings this problem into focus. Mr. Williams correctly notes that Milton criticism has constantly been subjected to "political bias," [3] the factor accounting in the eighteenth century for the divergent views of the Whig Addison and the Tory Johnson. In our own day, he argues, deep-rooted political prejudices have determined the views of critics like Tillyard, Grierson, and Whiting, all of whom regard *Paradise Lost* as a "defeatist" poem, a poem in which pessimism outweighs the solaces of the promised "New Heav'n, New Earth."

The assumption that *Paradise Lost* is pessimistic in meaning can be disproved on several scores. There is a growing body of specialized scholarship about the theme and motifs of the epic which shows them to be purely conventional, not the inventions of Milton, but rather his *selection from a vast body of material about the creation and fall* [italics mine]. The lines

> full of doubt I stand
> Whether I should repent mee now of sin
> By mee done

is what Lovejoy calls "the paradox of the fortunate fall." The notion is very ancient, he shows, that Adam's fall, by making possible

[3] "Conservative Critics of Milton," *Sewanee Review,* XLIX, No. 1, pp. 90 ff.

the mystery of the redemption, made possible a greater good than his remaining in obedience would have. It appears in the Roman Liturgy, in the Fathers, almost universally in Christian literature.[4]

The argument from "convention" is open to serious objections. That word "selection" alone should give pause to the critic who relies on sources and analogies in forming his judgment of an author's purpose. And "selection" here involves not merely the choice of this convention as against that convention, but the choice of the theme itself—the Fall of Man, the origin of evil. Then, too, the careful critic must decide whether or not Milton, once he has taken a convention from Christian tradition, gives it Christian treatment. Or to refine still further—is a convention common to the Roman liturgy and the Puritan sermon given a meaning which is at once Catholic and Protestant? Hilaire Belloc would say no. The argument from "convention" has in itself no critical value unless the problems of selection and treatment are fully understood, and in relation to the main purpose of the author.

Nevertheless, armed with Lovejoy's fortunate "paradox of the fortunate fall," Mr. Williams not only seeks to prove that *Paradise Lost* is optimistic, but also that criticism to the contrary is conservative, and even reactionary. Tillyard and Grierson fail to recognize that triumphant tone of *Paradise Lost* because both have "the widespread conservative distrust of revolutionary action by the masses."[5] If so, this is a distrust which they share with Milton himself, a distrust which characterizes *Paradise Lost* with its rigorous theology of elec-

[4] Williams, p. 96. He quotes from Arthur Lovejoy, "The Paradox of the Fortunate Fall," *ELH*, IV (1937), pp. 161–179.
[5] Williams, p. 103.

tion, its denial to the masses of men of that "Paradise within," the possession of the aristocratic few.

Tillyard, in commenting on the vision of the New Heaven and the New Earth vouchsafed to the "unparadised" Adam by Michael, says:

The comfort is nominal, the fundamental pessimism unmistakable. Milton seeks to comfort himself in an imagined new order, but it is not by any such distant possibility that his wound can be healed. For from his youth on Milton had nursed the hope that mankind would improve by its own resources. Just as he, by his will and energy, had cultivated his own mind, so could the rest of mankind, if it did but bend itself to the task, increase in mental well-being and happiness. His hopes, elated for a time by political events, were dashed far below their former lowest point, never to recover. Mankind would never in this world be any better; and Milton cannot be comforted. . . . He always felt within himself a standard, and a peculiarly exacting standard, of conduct which he had to obey. . . . It will be seen that only by considering this obedience and the pessimism together do we get at the meaning of *Paradise Lost*.[6]

Williams claims that Tillyard's conservatism (and one need not deny that Tillyard is a conservative) makes him incapable of understanding Milton's revolutionary faith in the masses, and Milton's revolutionary sense of triumph in the election of the few. Tillyard, being a conservative, cannot realize that the "salvation" of one Noah "outweighs the loss of thousands of weaker characters."[7] In other words, the "radical" critic must assume that Milton had a deep and abiding faith in "revolutionary action by the masses," and at the same time, with perfect consistency, a sense of joy in the salvation of the saintly few through faith rather than action, while the

[6] Tillyard, p. 287.
[7] Williams, p. 101.

mighty, numberless unregenerate (the masses) sink to perdition.

Surely there is a contradiction here, and an obvious one. I shall not labor the point. Mr. Williams' article shares the tendency of some self-consciously "leftist" criticism to arrive at radical judgments by the simple process of reversing the judgments of the conservatives. This is a dangerous procedure, and particularly so when the proof is not in the pudding but in the cook-book. We must evaluate the tone and purpose of *Paradise Lost* not in terms of epic convention (although a knowledge of literary tradition is always helpful) but in terms of the poem itself, and against the background of Milton's own intellectual and political development.

I have attempted to show in my second chapter that Milton was inherently aristocratic. He always believed that "Nature appoints that wise men should govern fools." This conviction led him not only to reject the hereditary monarchy of England, but also to reject the democratic theory of government. However radical he may seem in certain of his religious views, and in his ideas on divorce, he is never the political radical. He has little or nothing in common with a doctrinaire "leftist" like Lilburne; he is far "to the right" of even a moderate like Roger Williams.

The segregation of the spiritual and the secular, of which the separation of church and state is the outward and visible sign, penetrates to the foundations of Williams' thinking. Its primary object is to secure the absolute autonomy of the spiritual sphere. But it has a second result: it banishes from the secular sphere—and notably from the field of politics—every deduction made from theological data; it permits the complete secularization of the state and nullifies, so far as politics is concerned, the "aristocratic" principle inherent in Puritanism, with its sharp discrimination of saint and sinner and its dazzling hope that the Saints shall inherit the earth.

. . . The secularization of politics does not always lead necessarily to democracy, but it clears the way for democratic as for other developments. In the case of Puritanism, however, it removes from the field of politics the great obstacle to the necessary and unreserved addition of equality to liberty. And it releases to operate in that field, all those impulses—revolutionary, equalitarian, humanitarian—also inherent in Protestant Christianity and ready to emerge in the Puritan revolt. . . . In these developments Milton shares only within very definite limits. . . . In Milton the separation of church and state is not the symbol of a distinction which extends to the foundations of his thinking. . . . When the rights of the majority and the interests of the regenerate clash (as they patently do by 1660) Milton will not hesitate to sacrifice the former to the latter; he will sacrifice equality to liberty, and will take up the paradoxical position that in certain cases the regenerate may justly compel the unregenerate to be free—that is to accept the regenerate as their governors.[8]

Indeed, as I have pointed out,[9] he will subject the unregenerate to the rule, not of the spiritual aristocrats, but of the actual nobility. Milton's Platonic love of the philosopher-king, the "most worthy," symbolized for a time by Arthur and later by Cromwell, isolated him from the purely democratic currents of his age.[10]

[8] Woodhouse, "Milton, Puritanism, and Liberty," pp. 510–511. See also p. 98, n.

[9] Chap. II, pp. 59–61.

[10] Milton's aristocratic idealism was finally to separate him not only from the democratic current of the time (which was the minor current) but from the objective aims of the middle class. At the end he is Pope of his own church, and "Fuehrer" and sole member of his own political party. He has repudiated the people, the merchant class, and even Cromwell. It should be noted here that Cromwell's dictatorship reflects the inexorable movement of history. Cromwell, and not Lilburne, symbolized the progressive if ruthless advance. Milton's temporary support of the dictatorship involved a rationalization of idealist principles which had little relation to the realities of history. And Milton was never to understand objectively the failure of the Commonwealth because he had never understood objectively the significance of the Commonwealth.

On the face of it, this consideration might seem to prove, on other grounds, Arnold Williams' contention that the mood of *Paradise Lost* is optimistic. If the "optimism" of the epic is not "radical" perhaps it is aristocratic, flowing inevitably from Milton's basic and unchangeable theology of the Elect. Why should Milton feel gloom in an outcome which promises a "Paradise within" to the regenerate, however few? Why indeed was not such an outcome "the absolute culmination of all good"—the working out in cosmic terms of an aristocratic principle which he had always held?

In a sense *Paradise Lost* is the working out of the aristocratic principle in Milton's thought, and there can be no doubt that Milton *is* striving for an optimistic view of the universe. But one must remember here that the aristocratic element in Milton's earlier thought (of the Cambridge years through to the end of his period of service with the Cromwellian government) was imbedded in an intense nationalism, and his Puritanism was colored by Renaissance humanism, which as I have pointed out, inclined Milton to a belief in progress and perfectibility.[11] In *Paradise Lost,* Milton retains his aristocratic outlook but the other values of his once "hybrid culture" have been discarded.

I have offered sufficient evidence for Milton's nationalism and its descent from the Elizabethan patriotic tradition.[12] When one contrasts the patriotic fervor of passages in *Areopagitica* and *Of Reformation* with his estimate of England and Englishman after the Restoration, one is aware of the disappointed man whose brightest hopes have died. Once God had spoken "first to his Englishmen"[13] and had care

[11] Chap. II, pp. 39–40.
[12] Chap. II.
[13] *Areopagitica, S.M.,* p. 749.

to make that "noble and puissant nation" [14] first among the peoples of the earth, Milton had prepared to sing in "new and lofty measures" [15] of Christ's triumph and victory on earth "whereby this great and warlike nation, instructed and inured to the fervent and continual practice of truth and righteousness, may press on hard to that high and happy emulation to be found the soberest, wisest, and most Christian people at that day when Christ comes to judge all nations." [16] Milton's love of England, his identification of the Arthurian ideal with the history and the destiny of England, saved him at first from aristocratic detachment.

But note how diminished his nationalist feeling becomes:

For Britain, to speak a truth not often spoken, as it is a land fruitful enough of men stout and courageous, so it is naturally not over-fertile of men able to govern justly and prudently in peace, trusting only to their mother-wit. . . . Valeant indeed and prosperous to win a field; but to know the end and reason of winning unjudicious and unwise; in good and bad success alike unteachable.[17]

God and "his Englishmen" have parted company. By 1666 Milton had almost ceased to think of himself as an Englishman:

For the virtue you call statesmanship (but which I would rather have you call loyalty to my country), after captivating me with her fair-sounding name, has, so to speak, almost left me without a country. . . . One's country is wherever it is well with one.[18]

It is not so much that Milton came to lose faith in the people of England as it is that he came to realize that they existed.

[14] *Areopagitica, S.M.,* p. 750.
[15] *Of Reformation, S.M.,* p. 469.
[16] *Of Reformation,* p. 469.
[17] *History of Britain, P.W.,* V, p. 240.
[18] From a letter to Peter Heimbach, Tillyard, *Milton: Private Correspondence,* p. 51.

He quickly found them uncontrollable and unteachable. They are dumped from the abstract concept "the nation" (identified by tradition with the Arthurian ideal) into that impatient Puritan receptacle "the unregenerate." And with them went the hope of achieving on earth the Kingdom of Heaven.

In brief, "the Paradise within" is all that can be salvaged from the lost hope of a Paradise without, a Paradise that had been regarded by Milton not merely as an earthly possibility but as a definite national project.

There are other evidences of disillusionment in the later poems which cannot be disregarded here. The man who in the *Prolusions* and in *Areopagitica* had taken all knowledge for his province retracts in the words of Raphael:

> Such Commission from above
> I have receav'd, to answer thy desire
> Of knowledge within bounds; beyond abstain
> To ask, nor let thine own inventions hope
> Things not reveal'd, which th' invisible King
> Onely Omniscient hath supprest in Night,
> To none communicable in Earth or Heaven;
> Enough is left besides to search and know.
> But Knowledge is as food, and needs no less
> Her Temperance over Appetite, to know
> In measure what the mind may well contain,
> Oppresses else with Surfet, and soon turns
> Wisdom to Folly, as Nourishment to Winde.[19]

When Adam presses for more information than Gabriel has deemed it wise to give, the angel says:

> To ask or search I blame thee not, for Heav'n
> Is as the Book of God before thee set,
> Wherein to read his wondrous Works, and learne
> His Seasons, Hours, or Days, or Months, or Years;

[19] *P.L.*, vii, 118–130.

This to attain, whether Heav'n move or Earth,
Imports not, if thou reck'n right, the rest
From Man or Angel the great Architect
Did wisely to conceal, and not divulge
His secrets to be scann'd by them who ought
Rather admire; or if they list to try
Conjecture, he his Fabric of the Heav'ns
Hath left to their disputes, perhaps to move
His laughter at thir quaint Opinions.[20]

The Baconiàn spirit which had animated so much of Milton's opposition to the scholasticism of Cambridge is not only suppressed in favor of the Presbyterian virtues of obedience and temperance—but science is God's joke on man! This feeling may be due to political bitterness; it may reflect Milton's reaction to the spectacle of the scientist hobnobbing with the royalist after the Restoration. But one would infer from Milton's disavowal of the whole humanist tradition in *Paradise Regained* that this anti-scientific statement is part of a larger disillusionment with the hopes and methods of his revolutionary career. It is part of a general revulsion, a revulsion which comes out most clearly and most inclusively in the theory of history implicit in *Paradise Lost*.

By placing side by side the *History of Britain* and the concluding paragraphs of the pamphlet *Of Reformation*, Dr. H. Mutchmann is able to demonstrate the patriotic and optimistic nature of Milton's interest in history in the days when the Revolution had some hope of permanent success.[21] In *Of Reformation* Milton refers to the defeat of the Spanish Armada and the rise of the Britannic Nation at the command of Heaven. The dedication of Protestant England to "the fervent and continual practice of truth and righteousness has been

[20] *P.L.*, viii, 66–78.
[21] *Further Studies Concerning the Origins of Paradise Lost*, p. 5.

accomplished by the impetuous rage of five bloody inundations, and the succeeding sword of intestine war." [22] As
Mutchmann points out, the "five bloody inundations" may
be identified with the invasions of the Trojans; the Romans;
the Jutes, Angles, and Saxons; the Danes; and the Normans,
—described in the *History of Britain*. The implication in the
lines just quoted from *Of Reformation*, and the stated argument of the *History*, is that the invasions were directed by
God to punish and to civilize the inhabitants of the island
of Britain. Each invasion is regarded as a necessary step in the
education of the people to virtue.

The sixth invasion (the Spanish) is turned back by Provi-
dence. Manifestly, God is pleased with His people at last.
"The fervent and continual practice of truth has been accomplished." All is ready for the endless but joyous march
to an actual perfection. God functions through the historical
process, creating His new Heaven on the soil of England.
This is a clear-cut doctrine of perfectibility. Milton believed
that God assured progress in the real world, and in the
History of Britain he sought "to vindicate the ways of God
to Englishmen," [23] pointing the way to still higher national
achievements under the guidance of the Almighty. Indeed,
the *History* is regarded by Hanford as "a sort of commuta-
tion of Milton's earlier projects for a drama or an epic on a
British Legendary theme." [24]

However, the *History of Britain*, begun in 1646 and not
completed before 1655, has not quite the joyous confidence of
the Reformation pamphlet. The progressive theory of history is the same, but the optimism is grimmer. One gathers

[22] *Of Ref., S.M.*, p. 469.
[23] Mutchmann, p. 6.
[24] Hanford, p. 103.

that Milton is holding desperately to his faith in the Revolution and in the future of England, but the topical references inserted throughout the *History* indicate a growing uneasiness. At the beginning of Book III he bitterly denounces the Westminster Assembly for its dictatorial methods. He draws an ominous parallel between the England of his day and the state of Britain at the departure of the Romans. The Britons abused their new freedom:

> They seemed awhile to bestir themselves with a show of diligence in their new affairs, some secretly aspiring to the rule, others adoring the name of liberty, yet so soon as they felt by proof the weight of what it was to govern well themselves, and what was wanting in them, not stomach or the love of liscense, but the wisdom, the virtue, the labour to use and maintain true liberty, they soon remitted their heat and shrunk more wretchedly than before under a foreign yoke.[25]

England at the close of the Civil Wars is in a similar plight. Liberty had been put "like a bride" into the hands of Englishmen. Bribery, ambition, disregard for civil and religious liberty, were now threatening to bring the whole experiment to "ridiculous frustration."

> Thus they who of late were extolled as our greatest deliverers, and had the people wholly at their devotion, by so discharging their trust as we see, did only weaken and unfit themselves to be dispensers of what liberty they pretended, but unfitted also the people, now grown worse and more disordinate, to receive or digest any liberty at all. For stories teach us, that liberty sought out of season in a corrupt and degenerate age, brought Rome itself into farther slavery.[26]

This passage has a special significance. The people have "grown worse and more disordinate," and their search for

[25] *P.W.*, V, p. 241.
[26] *P.W.*, V, p. 239.

liberty in an age without true Christian leadership can only lead to disaster. In *Areopagitica* Milton had defended the right of the sects to nibble at truth. He had regarded their debates and their quarrels as the healthy ferment of an age awake. But the economic chaos attendant upon the Civil Wars gave a political coloring to the theology of important sections of a harassed people. The demand for political democracy was heard to rise above those quieter voices speaking for liberty of conscience. The leaderless masses, abandoning their quest for Christian liberty, were reaching out for an unregenerate liberty of the world which could profit them nothing. The age was losing its direction.

Milton concludes the *History of Britain* with the following words:

> If these were the causes of such misery and thraldom to our ancestors, with what better close can be concluded, than here in fit season to remember this age in the midst of our security, to fear from like vices, without amendment, the revolution of like calamities? [27]

Note that he speaks of "our security." The cause is not yet lost. In general, the work may be called "educational propaganda." God's concern with "his Englishmen" is revealed in terms of divine intervention in the historical process. But the accomplishment of the reign of God in England is not conceived here as inevitable or automatic. By displaying the past, Milton hopes to warn Englishmen against those abuses and perversions of liberty which destroy true freedom and delay the Millennium.

In *Paradise Lost* the doctrine of perfectibility in history has completely disappeared. Neither in the natural nor in the his-

[27] *P.W.*, V, p. 393.

torical process can perfection be achieved. God, in the end, must destroy His universe and create "new Heav'n, new Earth," a fit habitation for the Elect, who are rescued from nature and from history. The uneasiness, the fear that all was not well, which characterized the *History of Britain,* has become in *Paradise Lost* a conviction that man in society is a failure, incapable of ever achieving the rule of the Saints on earth.

The historical passages in *Paradise Lost,* those in which Michael unfolds for Adam a vision of the future of mankind, often parallel the topical references which I have noted in the *History of Britain.*

> Those whom last thou sawst
> In triumph and luxurious wealth, are they
> First seen in acts of prowess eminent
> And great exploits, but of true vertu void;
> Who having spilt much blood, and don much waste
> Subduing Nations, and achievd thereby
> Fame in the World, high titles, and rich prey,
> Shall change thir course to pleasure, ease, and sloth,
> Surfet, and lust, till wantonness and pride
> Raise out of friendship hostil deeds in Peace.
> The conquerd also, and enslav'd by Warr
> Shall with thir freedom lost all vertu loose
> And feare of God, from whom thir pietie feign'd
> In sharp contest of Battel found no aide
> Against invaders; therefore coold in zeale
> Thenceforth shall practice how to live secure,
> Worldlie or dissolute, on what thir Lords
> Shall leave them to enjoy; for th' Earth shall bear
> More than anough, that temperance may be tri'd:
> So all shall turn degenerate, all deprav'd,
> Justice and Temperance, Truth and Faith forgot;
> One Man except, the onely Son of light
> In a dark age.[28]

[28] *P.L.,* xi, 786–809.

Both the conquerors and the conquered, the rulers and the ruled are corrupt and incapable of practicing or understanding true liberty. "One Man except"—the Elect of his age—stands outside his-time and is plucked for eternity. The rest perish. Note, too, the austere reference to the goods of this world. The lost souls, instead of striving for spiritual perfection "practice how to live secure," little reckoning that the abundance of the earth is nothing more than a trap for the intemperate.

But whereas the *History of Britain* is written as a warning, *Paradise Lost* is written as an epitaph. Scene after scene of earthly frustration is unrolled before the horrified eyes of Adam. One by one the lonely Elect are extracted from doomed nature. Man need not struggle for a better society, nor expect any amelioration of his lot. God has abandoned the mass of men to the slow rot of the world. Only the tiny Elect of Noahs, Abrahams, and Miltons can hope, through the practice of "right reason," for the attainment of that "paradise within" which is the guarantee of eternal felicity.

It may be argued that such a belief is inherent in Christian thought,[29] and that the doctrine of the elect, inasmuch as it does not define rules of candidacy for the tiny society of saints, need be no cause for pessimism. Any man could (and very often did) consider himself of the elect. But it must be remembered that Milton was aware that the chosen number would be few, and what is more significant, he was aware that the patriotic aspirations of his revolutionary days were hopeless. England could not be saved. The Revolution could not be saved. The cause was lost. The Arthurian ideal, the concept of the man of virtue and "right reason" who could lead his people to the enjoyment of Christian liberty, was no

[29] See Arnold Williams, p. 102.

longer practicable for the real world. The ideal remained in
Milton's thought as the "absolute culmination of all good"
—but ripped out of the context of time and place. The ideal
was conceived at last *unhistorically,* "sub specie eternitatis."

That Milton had given up the good fight for a God-like
world is clear enough in another speech put into the mouth of
the Archangel Michael:

> Reason in man obscur'd, or not obey'd,
> Immediately inordinate desires
> And upstart Passions catch the Government
> From Reason, and to servitude reduce
> Man till then free. Therefore since hee permits
> Within himself unworthie Powers to reign
> Over free Reason, God in Judgement just
> Subjects him from without to violent Lords;
> Who oft as undeservedly enthrall
> His outward freedom; Tyrannie must be,
> Though to the Tyrant thereby no excuse.
> Yet somtimes Nations will decline so low
> From vertue, which is reason, that no wrong,
> But Justice, and some fatal curse annext
> Deprives them of thir outward libertie,
> Thir inward lost.[30]

The tyrants of the world, though themselves abhorrent, *rule
by God's will as a punishment to the unregenerate who have
thrown away their chance for salvation.* "Outward freedom" is lost because "inward freedom" was not cherished.
In the *History of Britain* Milton warned against the quest
for mere political and economic liberty "out of season." In
Paradise Lost he writes the final chapter of his history. His
warning has been disregarded. God who by "five bloody inundations" had sought to purge the English people of vanity
and spiritual sloth, had, by turning back the Spanish inva-

[30] *P.L.,* xii, 86–101.

sion, given a sign that the Millennium was at hand. The sign was ignored. And God withdrew from the historical process, leaving His people under "violent Lords."

This is pessimism, a pessimism, however, colored not with acquiescence but with vengeance. Milton sees Justice in the "Iron Heel" which God causes to descend upon the backs of the unregenerate. There is more than a hint of satisfaction in this, as there is in the prospect of the final destruction of a once indestructible matter. I think it can be shown that throughout *Paradise Lost* there is evidence of a vicarious exultation in sheer power.

It is my contention, then, that "the paradox of the fortunate fall" is not in itself a key to the mood and the emotional emphasis of the poem. A changed political outlook intrudes on the one constant element in Milton's theology—the doctrine of election. Poetically, this mood comes out clearly in the royalist imagery and symbolism, in the portrait of God as despot, not unlike in appearance and method to the "violent lords" who harass the unregenerate. This consideration brings me back logically to my original question: Why is God imagined as more autocratic than Charles? Why is Heaven made the very type of autocracy? Why was Milton not content to oppose the monarchies of earth with the "mild monarchy" of Christ, a monarchy exemplifying those principles of Christian liberty for which he had striven?

The Milton of *Paradise Lost* is a defeated political idealist. The Pauline doctrine of Christian liberty has been defeated by "realpolitik." Virtue and "right reason" may still be conceived as the principles of true freedom, but they *cannot win freedom for man*. Man who has forfeited his inner freedom deserves outward and physical tyranny. It serves him right! The abstract conception of Christian liberty is replaced by the Hebraic conception of the Almighty and jealous God enforcing obedience by fire, sword, and plague. The rational heaven of light and music is replaced by the heaven of steel and battle.

In discussing Milton's choice of biblical subject matter for his epic, Basil Willey has this to say:

> The traditional sources of poetry were running dry: mythologies were exploded and obsolete; no poet with Milton's passion for reality could pour all the energies of his nature into such moulds any longer. But there still remained one source . . . the Bible. Science might dismiss the old picture-thinking as phantasmal; Platonists might have striven to wipe off the gross dews of the imagination from the clear glass of the understanding; puritans might banish as carnal the poetry of ritual and symbol: all these and other agencies might be at work as they were, undermining and destroying older forms of religious and poetic experience; nevertheless here, in Scripture, God himself had condescended to be a poet and his divine revelation could therefore still be sung by a Milton with undamaged assurance.[31]

This is correct as far as it goes. The mythology of the past was under the scrutiny of the new scientific spirit. Abraham Cowley in the preface to his biblical epic *Davideis* specifically attacked the classical fables as obsolete, and urged poets of the time to make use of the "true" mythology of the Bible.[32]

Unquestionably, a consideration of the validity of the biblical material carried weight with Milton. But it must not be thought that Milton came suddenly to an awareness of the Bible as a literary source. His earlier poems from the *Nativity Ode* to *Lycidas* are full of biblical ideas and references. His doctrine of liberty is clearly influenced by the teaching of St. Paul. The significant fact is that his earlier religious writing

---

[31] *The Seventeenth Century Background*, pp. 228–229.
[32] *Poems of A. Cowley*, Cambridge English Classics, pp. 12 ff.

was colored predominantly by the New Testament, by the Christian rather than the Hebraic tradition. Even when he turns to the subject matter of the Old Testament, as he does between the years 1640 and 1642, it is apparent that he is imparting to it purely Christian significance. *The Cambridge Manuscript* contains four drafts for a play on the theme of the Fall. "The Persons" include Michael, Lucifer, Adam, Eve, Moses, Heavenly Love, Conscience, Mercy, Faith, Hope, Charity, Death, Labour, Sicknesse, Ignorance, and Feare. Neither God nor Christ is represented. They manifest themselves through the allegorical abstractions of Mercy and Justice.[33]

Of course a dramatist, and a Puritan one, could not represent the Deity on the stage. The fact that the Hebrew War-God does not appear in the "dramatis personae" is in itself of no significance. However, the drafts were made at the very time when Milton had decided to abandon his Arthurian epic because of distressing implications of Caroline royalism attached to the kingly symbol. Of the ninety-nine subjects listed for possible literary performance, only one is suggested for epic treatment—the Alfred episode. As I have pointed out, the interest in Alfred denotes a last attempt to find an epic king acceptable to Parliamentarian prejudice.[34] In view of Milton's long absorption in the project of the Arthurian epic, and in view of the fact that in a lengthy list of possible subjects only the disinfected Anglo-Saxon Alfred is mentioned as an epic hero, it seems fair to say that Milton has come to associate the epic form with the royalist hero, that he is extremely sensitive to the anti-royalist current of the time, and

[33] *Subjects for Poems and Plays from the Cambridge Manuscript, S.M.,* pp. 1128–1134.
[34] Chap. II, pp. 54–56.

that he turns to the dramatic form to escape an artistic predicament which he was not then prepared to solve in terms
of the epic. The mediaeval morality play provided him with
a medium through which he could express his idea of God
without confusing it with the prevalent notion of kingship.
Certainly the inference will stand, that at the moment Milton
felt forced to abandon his cherished Arthuriad he must have
been intensely aware of the implications of the royalist symbol. Nor can we readily explain the sudden dismissal of his
ambition to write the great English epic in favor of a play,
and preferably a play not on an English theme at all, unless
we recognize a conscious avoidance of royalist treatment.
Milton, *for the moment at least,* will drop the whole nationalist and patriotic tradition and write of the Fall of Man and
his salvation through the mercy of Christ—the central theme
of Christianity, vital to Milton, to all Englishmen, but relatively safe from controversy.[35]

There is no indication in these early drafts of the pessimism which overcasts *Paradise Lost.* This is the simple
Christian story of man's sin, man's repentance, God's forgive-
ness. I quote from Act V of the fourth draft:

Adam then and Eve return and accuse one another; but especially Adam lays the blame to his wife—is stubborn in his offence.
Justice appears, reasons with him, convinces him. The Chorus ad-
monishes Adam and bids him beware Lucifer's example of im-
penitence. The Angel is sent to banish them out of Paradise; but,

[35] I have stressed the political motivation behind Milton's choice of the
dramatic form because the temper of the time made such motivation decisive. However, I do not wish to deny Milton's long-standing interest in the
stage nor the possibility that his Italian trip quickened his enthusiasm for
the theatre. But we know that the plan for the patriotic epic was not far
from his thoughts during the sojourn in Italy. Although he may have been
excited by the Italian drama, it is doubtful indeed if literary fickleness alone
caused him to abandon the national epic and the national hero.

before, causes to pass before his eyes, in shapes, a masque of all the evils of this life and world. He is humbled, relents, despairs. At last appears Mercy, comforts him, promises him the Messiah; then calls in Faith, Hope, Charity; instructs him. He repents, gives God the glory, submits to his penalty. The Chorus briefly concludes.[36]

There is no hint of violent and vengeful destruction of the world here, no tyrannizing of the mass of men. The angry political overtones of *Paradise Lost* are the products of those later years in which Milton vainly sought "to free the land from this impertinent yoke of prelaty, under whose inquisitorious duncery no free and splendid wit can flourish" —the great task for which the plan to write an "Adam Unparadised" was set aside.

The representation of the acts of God by allegorical figures is reminiscent not only of such passages in the early poetry as

> Yea Truth, and Justice then
> Will down return to men,
> Orb'd in a Rain-bow; and, like glories wearing,
> Mercy will sit between,
> Thron'd in Celestiall sheen,
> With radiant feet the tissued clouds down stearing,[37]

or the description of Chastity in *Comus,* the whole conception of which is of a piece with the abstract Platonic manner in which Milton characterizes God in the poetry written before the Revolution. It is the conception of the idealist for whom God is reason, spirit, a "light unsufferable," the principle of harmony, the quality of mercy and justice—a being philosophical rather than anthropomorphic. It is within the tradition of Christian Platonism.

The God of *Paradise Lost* is the God of Moses:

[36] *S.M.*, pp. 1133–1134.
[37] *Nativity Ode*, lines 141–146.

The Lord is a man of war: the Lord is his name.[38]

Thy right hand, O Lord, is become glorious in power; thy right hand, O Lord, hath dashed in pieces the enemy.

And in the greatness of thine excellency thou hast overthrown them that rose up against thee; thou sentest forth thy wrath, which consumed them as stubble.[39]

The people of Milton's world are the people of Israel:

They have corrupted themselves, their spot is not the spot of his children.[40]

They sacrificed unto devils, not to God; to gods whom they knew not, to new gods that came newly up, whom your fathers feared not.[41]

For they are a nation void of counsel, neither is there any understanding in them.[42]

They are punished by the angry God:

I will hide my face from them, I will see what their end shall be: for they are a very froward generation, children in whom is no faith.[43]

I will heap mischiefs upon them: I will spend my arrows upon them.[44]

To me belongeth vengeance, and recompence; their foot shall slide in due time: for the day of their calamity is at hand, and the things that shall come upon them make haste.[45]

The Milton of *Paradise Lost* is not the Christian saint but the Hebrew prophet, not unlike the lonely Moses, shut out from the Promised Land, calling in agony and frustration for the vengeance of God upon a sinful, ignorant, and treacherous

[38] *Exodus* 15: 3.
[39] *Ex.* 15: 6–7.
[40] *Deuteronomy* 32: 5.
[41] *Deut.* 32: 17.
[42] *Deut.* 32: 28.
[43] *Deut.* 32: 20.
[44] *Deut.* 32: 23.
[45] *Deut.* 32: 35.

people, a people which had betrayed its promised destiny.

A recognition of the necessity of power in politics had come gradually to Milton. The spirit of true liberty which Milton thought would fall like bright dawn over England, transforming the social and political landscape, appeared only to the few. And as the majority of men were not moved by liberty at all, Milton was to adopt "the paradoxical position that in certain cases the regenerate may justly *compel* the unregenerate to be free." [46] The ideal seems lost without the power to impose it.

There can be no doubt that Milton had at first regarded Cromwell as an Arthurian knight in shining armor, able by very perfection of soul to draw about him the great mass of Englishmen. "For he was a soldier disciplined to perfection in the knowledge of himself. He had either extinguished or by habit learned to subdue the whole host of vain hopes, fears, and passions which subdue the soul." [47] He was "a very parfait, gentil knight."

Indeed, Milton seems to regard the panegyric of Cromwell in the *Second Defense* as the culmination of his plans for an epic on a national theme. "It will be sufficient, either for my justification or apology, that I have heroically celebrated at least one exploit of my countrymen; I pass by the rest, for who could recite the achievements of a whole people?" [48]

Cromwell is clearly Arthur, and the "whole people," that great unindividualized lump of nationhood, is elevated with him and by him to the shining levels of freedom.

Do you then, sir, continue your course with the same unrivalled magnanimity; it sits well upon you;—to you your country owes its

[46] Woodhouse, "Milton, Puritanism, and Liberty," p. 512; italics mine.
[47] *P.W.*, I, p. 285.
[48] *P.W.*, I, p. 299.

liberties; nor can you sustain a character at once more momentous and more august than that of the author, the guardian, and the preserver of our liberties; and hence you have not only *eclipsed the achievement of all our kings, but even those which have been fabled of our heroes.*[49]

Cromwell is a greater king, even surpassing Arthur. He guarantees the liberty of the whole people with "magnanimity." The passage is in effect a "plea for the application of principles in the administration of the state without which the English people will slip back into the slavery from which they have risen." [50] The responsibility for the preservation of liberty rests with Cromwell. Unfortunately for Milton's vision of magic leadership, of a national ethic and consciousness embodied and preserved in the person of a single leader, Cromwell found it necessary to protect liberty by butchering the Irish, smashing the Levellers, and overawing opposition, actual or incipient, by the use or the threat of armed force. Over a society divided against itself into groups, some of which sought sheer profit, some of which sought actual political democracy, some of which even questioned the sacred God-given right of private property, Cromwell ruled as a "strong man."

Milton did not always approve, but he was impressed. There was no other way. One may "justly compel the unregenerate to be free." One must drive them back to their destiny. One must *force* them from their new, unhallowed gods before it was too late.

And when it *was* too late the power-politician in Milton was stronger than the Platonic idealist,—that whimsical little fellow who had stubbed his toe on the hard rock of secular

[49] *P.W.*, I, pp. 289–290; italics mine.
[50] *Handbook*, p. 101.

reality. Like Moses, Milton must go down to the foolish, evil, irresponsible masses and destroy them. For theirs is the blame. They had the power of choice. Their just reward is the tyranny of kings, and final and utter destruction.

Milton's despotic God is the sick man's dream of strength, the poetic sublimation of anger, frustration, and vengeance. For such a theme royalist treatment was inevitable. There was no other idiom for the representation of sheer power. Fortunately, the Hebrew King of Kings could be distinguished at least intellectually from the Kings of England. In 1642 Milton may have hesitated to make an epic hero of the King of Heaven, but at that time Milton's conception of God was Christian rather than Hebraic, idealist rather than anthropomorphic—and because of the coincidence of his Arthurian interests and plans he was then too acutely aware of the Stuart implications of a kingly hero. Given the Hebraic rather than the Christian temper, given the poetic impulse to create an image in terms of power politics which could transcend and destroy thrones, peoples, worlds—Milton could only be drawn to "the one source" which remained valid for the Puritan anti-royalist mind, the Old Testament, the King-God of Moses.

But while it is easy enough to make a clear intellectual distinction between the royalism of God and the royalism of Charles, it is not so easy to make a poetic distinction, particularly if the poet happens to be steeped in the royalist idiom of the English tradition.

There can be no doubt that Milton did attempt to extricate his Hebraic royalism from any association with national royalist values.[51] In several important passages of *Paradise Lost*

[51] The subject-matter of *Paradise Lost* invites Milton to draw his royalist allusions from scriptural sources and from his vast knowledge of ancient

he repudiates the Arthurian epic, the English Court, and the romantic trappings of a once cherished tradition. And what is equally significant, he presents his aristocratic Elect, the brands plucked from the burning, not as thinly disguised Spenserian knights, but as simple virtuous citizens scornful of earthly kings.

Note his rejection of the kingly epic in Book IX. He states flatly that he is

> Not sedulous by Nature to indite
> Warrs, hitherto the onely Argument
> Heroic deem'd, chief maistrie to dissect
> With long and tedious havoc fabl'd Knights
> In Battels feign'd; the better fortitude
> Of Patience and Heroic Martyrdom
> Unsung; or to describe Races and Games,
> Or tilting Furniture, emblazon'd Shields,
> Impreses quaint, Caparisons and Steeds;
> At Joust and Torneament; then marshal'd Feast
> Serv'd up in Hall with Sewers, and Seneshals;
> The skill of Artifice or Office mean,
> Not that which justly gives Heroic name
> To Person or to Poem. Mee of these
> Nor skilld nor studious, higher Argument
> Remaines.[52]

history and literature. That he does not always do so I shall show. The chivalric tradition constantly intrudes. However it must be recognized that Milton cannot save himself from English royalist associations by confining his allusions to ancient kings. The idea of kingship could not be easily dissociated from contemporary example. Throughout his pamphlets, Milton had attacked kings whenever and wherever they were to be found—even in Israel. In *The Ready and Easy Way* he wrote: "God in much displeasure gave a king to the Israelites, and imputed it a sin to them that they sought one; but Christ apparently forbids his disciples to admit of any such heathenish government" (*S.M.*, p. 903). For Milton a king was a king, and a republic a republic, whether in England, Israel, Greece, or Rome. For him ancient kings were as English as Tamburlaine was English for Marlowe.

[52] Lines 27–43.

The passage shows that he *is* "skilld," and that he has been "studious." He revels in these sounds and shapes which he must piously reject. His dismissal of the royalist epic with its Stuart and Tudor associations is merely formal and arbitrary. It will not save his poem from a riot of confusion.

In other passages he clearly associates evil with the courts and kingdoms of the world. Thus, of Belial:

> In Courts and Palaces he also Reigns
> And in luxurious Cities, where the noyse
> Of riot ascends above thir loftiest Towrs,
> And injury and outrage.[53]

The following is a bitter reference to the court of Charles II:

> Still govern thou my Song
> *Urania,* and fit audience find, though few.
> But drive farr off the barbarous dissonance
> Of *Bacchus* and his Revellers, the Race
> Of that wilde Rout that tore the *Thracian* Bard
> In *Rhodope,* where Woods and Rocks had Eares
> To Rapture, till the savage clamor dround
> Both Harp and Voice; nor could the Muse defend
> Her Son.[54]

In Book XI the Archangel Michael takes Adam to a hilltop similar to the one from which Satan was to tempt Christ with a show of "all Earths Kingdomes and thir Glory." This gives Milton an opportunity to display the exciting but futile vainglory of regal splendor:

> His Eye might there command wherever stood
> City of old or modern Fame, the Seat
> Of mightiest Empire, from the destind Walls
> Of *Cambalu,* seat of *Cathaian Can*
> And *Samarchand* by *Oxus, Temirs* Throne

[53] I, 497–500.
[54] VII, 30–38.

To *Paquin* of *Sinæan* Kings, and thence
To *Agra* and *Lahor* of great *Mogul*.[55]

The passage is a *tour-de-force* of sheer erudition. Milton's long-acquired knowledge of kings, emperors, tsars, sultans, and his love of great names, mighty sounds, suggestive of barbaric pomp and circumstance, are deliberately introduced into a passage meant to negate the very glories which are invoked. It is a skillful poetic trick, this, of getting the sensation while denying the sense, of eating the cake without having it. The angel does not show Adam what Milton has shown us. He saves his eyes for "nobler sights." [56] The digression has been given to deny "all Earths Kingdomes and thir Glory." Yet Milton is to adorn his Heaven with the despised grandeur of earth. The purely decorative confusion into which he is forced is illustrated in Book I. The fallen Angels are building the palaces of hell:

> Let none admire
> That riches grow in Hell; that soyle may best
> Deserve the pretious bane. And here let those
> Who boast in mortal things, and wondring tell
> Of *Babel,* and the works of *Memphian* Kings,
> Learn how thir greatest Monuments of Fame,
> And Strength and Art are easily outdone
> By Spirits reprobate, and in an hour
> What in an age they with incessant toyle
> And hands innumerable scarce perform.[57]

The riches and beauty of earthly kingdoms are proper to the soil of Hell. But Hell is a copy of Heaven, designed by the selfsame architect who had made Heaven glorious. When the infernal palaces and temples had been erected

[55] Lines 385–391. The whole passage to line 422 is important for this point.
[56] Line 411.
[57] Lines 690–699.

The hasty multitude
Admiring enter'd, and the work some praise
And some the Architect: *his hand was known*
In Heav'n by many a Towred structure high,
Where Scepter'd Angels held thir residence,
And sat as Princes, whom the supreme King
Exalted to such power. . . .
Nor was his name unheard or unador'd
In ancient *Greece;* and in *Ausonian* land
Men called him *Mulciber.*[58]

It is difficult to damn the vanity of earth by making it the mirror of Heaven. Milton's insatiate desire for symbols of splendor and power quite obliterated conscious intellectual distinctions.

In Book III he describes a company of Catholic "Eremits and Friers, White, Black and Grey," wandering in Limbo:

A violent cross wind from either Coast
Blows them transverse ten thousand Leagues awry
Into the devious Air; then might ye see
Cowles, Hoods and Habits with their wearers tost
And flutterd into Raggs, then Reliques, Beads,
Indulgences, Dispenses, Pardons, Bulls,
The sport of Winds.[59]

Here is the typical Puritan hatred for Catholicism with its "reliques" and "beads," its ritual and symbol.

Yet Milton's Heaven when it is not an armoury is a Catholic cathedral. It certainly never resembles the conventicle.

See Father, what first fruits on Earth are sprung
From thy implanted Grace in Man, these Sighs
And Prayers, which in this Golden Censer, mixt
With Incense, I thy Priest before thee bring.[60]

[58] Lines 730–740; italics mine.
[59] Lines 487–493.
[60] XI, 22–25.

Milton's theology is not consistent with his interior decoration. Perhaps the sharpest and most confusing contradiction occurs in those descriptions of Heaven clearly derived from the English epic tradition of "tinsel trappings," "gorgious knights," and jousts and tournaments.

> On such day
> As Heav'ns great Year brings forth, th' Empyreal Host
> Of Angels by Imperial summons call'd,
> Innumerable before th' Almighties Throne
> Forthwith from all the ends of Heav'n appeerd
> Under thir Hierarchs in orders bright
> Ten thousand thousand Ensignes high advanc'd,
> Standards, and Gonfalons twixt Van and Reare
> Streame in the Aire, and for distinction serve
> Of Hierarchies, of Orders, and Degrees.[61]

This is an Arthurian Heaven. It comes from *The Faerie Queene* rather than from the Bible. The passage is full of associations national and political which Milton has specifically rejected as unfit for "higher argument."

But in a passage from the same book Milton is at some pains to contrast the "tedious" splendor of a Royal Progress with the simple unostentatious perfection of the Angel Gabriel:

> In himself was all his state,
> More solemn than the tedious pomp that waits
> On Princes, when thir rich Retinue long
> Of Horses led, and Grooms besmeard with Gold
> Dazles the croud, and sets them all agape.[62]

One is scarcely less confused when Adam's next angelic visitor appears as follows:

[61] V, 583–591.
[62] Lines 353–357.

Th' Arch-Angel soon drew nigh,
Not in his shape Celestial, but as Man
Clad to meet Man; over his lucid Armes
A militarie Vest of purple flowd
Livelier than *Meliboean*, or the graine
Of *Sarra*, worn by Kings and Hero's old
In time of Truce; *Iris* had dipt the wooff;
His starrie Helme unbuckl'd shew'd him prime
In Manhood where Youth ended; by his side
As in a glistening *Zodiac* hung the Sword.[63]

Michael more than outdoes the "tedious pomp of Princes."
What are we to feel? That the splendor of kings is a vanity
to dazzle the stupid gaping crowd? Or that it is a positive
value? Those critics who regard the poem as a gallery of pic-
tures, and those critics who confine their interest to an interpretation of the thought, may not be concerned with this
problem. But Milton was. Note his explanatory comment that
Michael's garb is not "Celestial," but a concession to Man.
Milton is certainly not thinking here of Adam who was
scarcely accustomed by experience to such displays. Rather,
Milton is trying to square his description of Michael with
previous descriptions of worldly pomp. Michael does not appear in the simple garb of the "sociably mild" [64] Raphael because he comes not to praise God but to blame Adam. He
comes to drive Adam from Paradise. His is a mission of power
for which the warrior costume is appropriately symbolic.
And so Milton consciously justifies his use of the symbolism
of power, and seeks to save himself from inconsistency and
from seeming to identify the angel with the shape of "Kings
and Hero's old."

This struggle for consistency comes out most clearly in

[63] XI, 238–247.
[64] XI, 234.

Raphael's preamble to his description of the war in Heaven, a description which, as Mutchmann shows,[65] is drawn from contemporary accounts of the defeat of the Spanish Armada:

> High matter thou injoinst me, O prime of men,
> Sad task and hard, for how shall I relate
> To human sense th' *invisible exploits*
> *Of warring Spirits;* how without remorse
> The ruin of so many glorious once
> And perfet while they stood; how last unfould
> The secrets of another world, perhaps
> Not lawful to reveal? yet for thy good
> This is dispenc't, and what surmounts the reach
> Of human sense, *I shall delineate so,*
> *By lik'ning spiritual to corporal forms*
> As may express them best, *though what if Earth*
> *Be but the shaddow of Heav'n, and things therein*
> *Each to other like, more then on earth is thought?* [66]

This is indeed evasive. The reader is asked to make a clear intellectual distinction between the powers of Heaven and the powers of earth, between the spiritual and the real. But the emotional response of the reader must depend on a sympathy for the earthly suggestions of power and grandeur which follow. Perhaps, Milton is forced to say, Heaven and earth are more alike than men have imagined. He is forced to say this not only because his values will be confused if the theological distinction between spirit and matter is taken too seriously, if it be felt that the vainglory of earth taints the glory of Heaven, but also because he has already averred that Heaven's towers were built by the same architect who later practised his lovely craft in Greece and the "Ausonian land."

[65] *Milton's Projected Epic on the Rise and Future Greatness of the Britannic Nation,* Tartu, 1936.
[66] V, 563–575; italics mine.

Milton has beautified the City of God with "the glory that was Greece" and he cannot afford, nor does he desire, to reduce the imaginative illusion. But, as the quoted passage shows, he is conscious of a highly complex problem of representation. In the famous Invocation to Light at the beginning of Book III, he returns for a moment to a description of God in the Platonic-Christian tradition of his early poetry:

Hail Holy light, ofspring of Heav'n first-born,
Or of th' Eternal Coeternal beam
May I express thee unblam'd? *since God is light,*
And never but in unapproached light
Dwelt from Eternitie, dwelt then in thee,
Bright effluence of bright essence increate.
Or hear'st thou rather pure Ethereal stream,
Whose Fountain who shall tell? before the Sun,
Before the Heavens thou wert, and at the voice
Of God, as with a Mantle didst invest
The rising world of waters dark and deep. . . .
                    Thus with the year
Seasons return, but not to me returns
Day, or the sweet approach of Ev'n or Morn,
Or sight of vernal bloom, or Summers Rose,
Or flocks, or herds, or human face divine;
But cloud in stead, and ever-during dark
Surrounds me, from the chearful waies of men
Cut off. . . .
So much the rather thou Celestial light
Shine inward, and the mind through all her powers
Irradiate, there plant eyes, all mist from thence
Purge and disperse, that I may see and tell
Of things invisible to mortal sight.[67]

The passage embodies the first of the great personal utterances which recur at intervals throughout *Paradise Lost* and constitute a lyric thread interweaving itself with the objective narrative. The pathos of blindness, the consoling love of beauty, the thirst for fame, the consciousness of precious inward vision vouchsafed for

[67] Lines 1–55; italics mine.

the deprivation of outward Light are expressed with consummate eloquence.[68]

As Hanford says, the invocation is quite outside "the objective narrative." This God of Light, to whom Milton turns in his blindness and his despair, is not the Power-God who will smite the unregenerate. He is the God of the Elect. He is the God of the *Nativity Ode*, "bright essence." Nothing more clearly reveals the dominant vengeance motif of *Paradise Lost* than this private God of Milton's who

> never but in unapproached light
> Dwelt from Eternitie.

The royalist power imagery *within* the "objective narrative," the crowns, the sceptres, the cannon, the feudal ritual of heaven, the whole grandiose effect of might, pomp, and terror, is a poetic sublimation of that earthly tyranny which man deserves. But after the unregenerate world has burned to ash, and God has created "New Heav'n and new Earth," the Platonic ideal will be realized again. In the words of God to the Son,

> the just shall dwell
> And after all thir tribulations long
> See golden days, fruitful of golden deeds,
> With Joy and Love triumphing, and fair Truth.
> Then thou thy regal Scepter shalt lay by,
> For regal Scepter then no more shall need,
> God shall be All in All.[69]

In the final "classless society" of the Elect, the coercive state shall "wither away." After the last spark of the condemned world has turned to ash, the royalist symbol can be dropped, the crown dissolved, the fleshless spiritual values of Truth and

[68] *Hanford,* pp. 179–180.
[69] III, 335–341.

Joy and Love will be restored. The value of the royalist symbol is merely punitive. Speed the time when it can be dispensed with, the job done! [70]

It should be apparent now that Milton's royalism is an involved and difficult thing. Careful distinctions have been made between the King-God of the Hebrews and the Kings of Earth. Milton is aware of the dangerous connotations of royalism. But his still profound fascination with the heroic epic, and the poetic necessity of creating heavenly symbols of power which can be understood and felt, obliterates the conscious distinction between Heaven and earth. As I have pointed out, the vanity and evil of earthly monarchies are suggested in poetic terms indistinguishable from those which suggest the splendor of Heaven. By inserting signposts, by telling us when to feel "This is vain" and "This is glorious," Milton seeks to keep his distinctions clear, to keep God innocent of associations with British royalism. That he fails is evident, and that he is conscious of the dilemma in which he finds himself is equally evident.

It should be observed that in the Invocation to Book III Milton carefully avoids any association of the abstract God of Light with the royalist God of the narrative. In the early poetry, written before the English Revolution at a time when

[70] This idea, clearly stated in the quoted passage from Book III, is contradicted again in Book XII. The biblical story demands that Christ descend from the royal David. Michael is indignant that usurpers steal the sceptre

> and regard not *Davids* Sons,
> Then loose it to a stranger, that the true
> Anointed king *Messiah* might be born
> Barr'd of his right. [357–360.]

Christ has been *cheated* of worldly glory and position. Yet he shall recover his kingliness and ascend "the throne hereditarie" [370]. There is no suggestion here that he will eventually put aside royalism. "Of his Reign shall be no end" [330]. The biblical tradition offers as many difficulties for Milton as the Spenserian.

Milton's indifference to the Stuarts was matched by his deference for rank, the Platonic images are usually given a royalist setting—"The Prince of Light," the "far-beaming blaze
of majesty." The symbols merge. But in *Paradise Lost* Milton introduces the Platonic concept to *cancel* the worldly
appearance of God in his just moment of anger. The royalist
demeanor is necessary but temporary. God will revert as soon
as possible to "bright essence." Indeed it is hinted, sometimes
even stated, that God is never King, his warriors never warriors, his palaces never palaces. The whole picture is simply
a reduction to the absurdity of human understanding.

What precisely then, is the meaning, the reference value,
of royalism in *Paradise Lost?* God is King. He is not to be
confused with the kings of earth. *He is precisely like the kings
of earth.* He is not king at all! Kingship is the tyranny of the
wicked over the wicked. Kingship is the power of God. Kingship is not desirable in itself, and will cease to exist *even metaphorically* in the final dwelling-place of the blessed spirits.
There are, it is true, theological and political justifications for
these shifts of value in the poem. But there is no poetic justification. There can be none. A single symbol, appearing at
three different levels, with three separate connotations and
but one form, provides a difficult problem in manipulation
for any poet. *And the problem becomes insoluble when one
connotation, one set of traditional values attached to the symbol, is in sharp contradiction with another.* Logically, it might
almost be said that the earthly and heavenly connotations of
kingship cancel each other into the kingless abstraction that
is to represent the "New Heav'n." By making use of the only
idiom which could convey the sense of might and vengeance,
the anti-royalist Milton had to employ the tricks of the contortionist in order not to identify the Almighty (and him-

self) with the royalist tradition and with royalist sympathies. John Donne could frankly and unashamedly make the Court of Heaven a replica of the Court of England. But now a direct equation of royalism and worth was impossible. In *Paradise Lost* the royalist symbol consistently suggests no value except power. A confusion of other values inevitably results. This confusion is most pronounced in the treatment of characters where clear-cut distinctions of good and evil are necessary.

In the vision of the future vouchsafed to Adam by the Archangel, Milton is at some pains to present his ideal characters, those who dare "single to be just," against a hostile and evil background of "arms, fierce faces threatening Warr," tournaments, heralds, and the like. Elijah defies the monarchies of the world. Noah, in a significant image, is the "onely Son of light in a dark age." These just men, of course, embody the Platonic-Arthurian virtues. They are citizen Arthurs. Poetically, the Arthurian symbol is split, divided against itself. The "sons of light" oppose the kings and the warriors. The purely moral element in the Arthurian symbol is separated from, and confronts the picturesque. Elijah

> spake much of Right and Wrong,
> Of Justice, of Religion, Truth and Peace.[71]

But

> in those dayes Might onely shall be admir'd
> And Valour and Heroic Vertu call'd;
> To overcome in Battel, and subdue
> Nations, and bring home spoils with infinite
> Man-slaughter, shall be held the highest pitch
> Of human Glorie, and for Glorie done
> Of triumph, to be styl'd great Conquerours,

[71] XI, 666–667.

Patrons of Mankind, Gods, and Sons of Gods,
Destroyers rightlier call'd and Plagues of men.[72]

High titles, fame, conquest, knightly encounters—the
"Plagues of men." The chivalric aspect of the Arthurian symbol is discarded as not merely worthless but *evil*.

Yet Heaven is presented as chivalric, with its "Hierarchs,"
"Ensignes high advanced," its feudal ritual, its Roman Catholic altar and incense. What is even more disturbing, Hell is
chivalric. The fallen angels stand

> in guise
> Of warriers old with order'd Spear and Shield
> Awaiting what command thir mighty Chief
> Had to impose: He through the armed Files
> Darts his experienc't eye, and soon traverse
> The whole Battalion views, thir order due,
> Thir visages and stature as of Gods,
> Thir number last he summs. And now his heart
> Distends with pride, and hardning in his strength
> Glories: For never since created man,
> Met such imbodied force, as nam'd with these
> Could merit more then that small infantry
> Warr'd on by Cranes: though all the Giant brood
> Of Phlegra with th' Heroic Race were joyn'd
> That fought at Theb's and Ilium, on each side
> Mixt with auxiliar Gods; and what resounds
> *In Fable or Romance of Uthers Son*
> *Begirt with British and Armoric Knights.*[73]

One might expect that if knights, warriors and conquerors
are the evil "Plagues of men," the warriors of hell would be
evil indeed, and their trappings the very symbol of evil. Such
is not the case. The allusion to British fable is meant to con-
jure up positive visions of grandeur. It is given a favourable

[72] XI, 689-698.
[73] I, 564-581; italics mine.

connotation. The fallen angels are still angels and dressed for heaven. Satan

> Stood like a Towr; his form had not yet lost
> All her Original brightness, nor appear'd
> Less then Arch Angel ruind, and th' excess
> Of Glory obscur'd.[74]

There are, however, differences between the leaders of hell. Curiously enough Belial, who, we are told, was later to pollute the courts and palaces of earth, is not regal at all. He "counsel'd ignoble ease, and peaceful sloth." [75] He is not a knight. He is not valorous. He is contemptible, and Milton makes him so quite deliberately. But if his counsel had been accepted Adam would not have been visited by evil. On the other hand, Beelzebub, who urged war against God through the seduction of Man, *is* regal:

> with grave
> Aspect he rose, and in his rising seem'd
> A Pillar of State; deep on his Front engraven
> Deliberation sat and publick care;
> And Princely counsel in his face yet shon,
> Majestick though in ruin.[76]

The vigorous and powerful leaders are princely and majestic in appearance, most like the Potentates of Heaven. And yet Beelzebub gives "devilish counsel" [77] inspired by the "Author of all ill." [78]

The royal treatment of Satan and Beelzebub, and the disparagement of the weaker characters like Belial, have provided the "Satanists" with an argument in support of their

[74] I, 591–594.
[75] II, 227.
[76] II, 300–306.
[77] II, 379.
[78] II, 381.

contention that Milton is of the devil's party without knowing it. As I have stated, scholars, particularly those who have
made a careful study of Milton's thought, no longer toy with
the notion that Satan is, by accident or design, the hero of
the poem. Poetically, however, there is a confusion which has
exposed the poem to the Satanic interpretation. Tillyard, in
discussing the "unconscious meaning" of *Paradise Lost,* repudiates the Satanic theory, but admits that

The character of Satan expressed, as no other character or act of
feature of the poem does, something in which Milton believed very
strongly: heroic energy. Not that this is a quality confined to Satan;
how could it be, when it is the very essence of Milton's nature? [79]

The "heroic energy" of Satan is a necessary foil to the greater
power of God. The enemies of God must be worthy of his
steel. Consequently, the most devilish have to be presented as
the most noble. The less dangerous of the fallen angels are
ignoble. It is significant that not until after the temptation of
Adam, and after the description of the war in Heaven—in
other words, *after the royalist symbolism of power has served
its purpose of providing dramatic opposition to God,*—is
Hell deprived of its royalist appearance and presented in images of evil. Satan returns from his single daring war against
God and man. His "Princes, Potentates, Warriors" rush to see

> In Triumph issuing forth thir glorious Chief;
> They saw, but other sight instead, a crowd
> Of ugly Serpents; horror on them fell,
> And horrid sympathie; for what they saw,
> They felt themselvs now changing; down thir arms,
> Down fell both Spear and Shield, down they as fast,
> And the dire hiss renew'd, and the dire form
> Catcht by Contagion, like in punishment,
> As in thir crime. Thus was th' applause they meant

[79] *Milton*, p. 277.

> Turnd to exploding hiss, triumph to shame
> Cast on themselves from thir own mouths.[80]

For Satan, who had once stood like a tower of majesty, appears to his followers as a serpent:

> His Visage drawn he felt to sharp and spare,
> His Armes clung to his Ribs, his Leggs entwining
> Each other, till supplanted down he fell
> A monstrous Serpent on his Belly prone,
> Reluctant, but in vaine, *a greater power*
> *Now rul'd him,* punish't in the shape he sin'd,
> According to his doom.[81]

The struggle of Satan with God has been a struggle for power.

> Lifted up so high
> I sdeind subjection, and thought one step higher
> Would set me highest.[82]

> To bow and sue for grace
> With suppliant knee, and deifie his power
> Who from the terrour of this Arm so late
> Doubted his Empire, that were low indeed.[83]

The illusion of Satanic power and majesty must be retained until after we have been shown the full might of Heaven in action, until the sense of greater power has been realized.

After the battle of Heaven has raged back and forth without conclusion God speaks to his Son:

> Two dayes are therefore past, the third is thine;
> For thee I have ordain'd it, and thus farr
> Have sufferd, that the Glorie may be thine
> Of ending this great Warr, since none but Thou
> Can end it. *Into thee such Vertu and Grace*
> *Immense I have transfus'd, that all may know*
> *In Heav'n and Hell thy Power above compare,*

[80] X, 537–547.
[81] X, 511–517; italics mine.
[82] IV, 49–51.
[83] I, 111–114.

And this perverse Commotion governd thus,
To manifest thee *worthiest to be Heir*
Of all things, to be Heir and to be King
By Sacred Unction, thy deserved right.
Go then thou Mightiest in thy Fathers might,
Ascend my Chariot, guide the rapid Wheeles
That shake Heav'ns basis, bring forth all my Warr,
My Bow and Thunder, my Almightie Arms
Gird on, and Sword upon thy puissant Thigh;
Pursue these sons of Darkness, drive them out
From all Heav'ns bounds into the utter deep.[84]

The "Prince of Light" is here the warrior-king armed with his Father's might. He is distinguished intellectually but not poetically from Satan by the signposts of virtue, grace, worth. Satan's royalism is similar in kind to the Son's though less in degree. The final conflict between the two is the military dress rehearsal of that might in action which will one day hurl its spears on the unregenerate of the world, destroying even the world itself. The conquest of majesty by majesty is the apotheosis of illimitable power. It is the central theme of the poem.

We have seen the Sons of Light represented as admirable in contradistinction to the champions of "Heroick Vertu" and conquest—the "Plagues of men." We have admired Satan above the "ignoble" Belial for the possession of this same "Heroick Vertu." We admire emotionally what we know intellectually to be "devilish" in order that we may more greatly admire superior force when it strikes. The stage is set for the supreme exaltation of power. All the moral and social implications of the royalist symbol are confused and lost. On occasion evil is good, good is evil.

The real paradox of *Paradise Lost* is not "fortunate." Whereas Shakespeare's king had divinity in him, a divinity

[84] VI, 699–716; italics mine.

created in the image of a unified society, Milton's divinity is
king to destroy a divided unregenerate society, a king to
destroy kings as well as people. Whereas in Shakespeare splendor and might are incidental to the "inner" value of the royalist symbol ("Take physic, pomp"), in *Paradise Lost* moral
values have to be carefully detached from the royalist symbol, leaving it nothing but the suggestion of power. By deliberately inserting moral judgments and distinctions, Milton
seeks arbitrarily to control the connotation of the royalist
symbol. In other words he strives to deny contemporary political reference to his royalist symbol when it is used to
represent God, but to utilize such reference when the symbol
represents the tyrannies of earth.

In the early poems Milton's "complimentary references" to
the idea of royalty are perfunctory and suggest no more than
rank. Milton's society then did not contradict, even if it did
not refresh, the aristocratic values inherited from the Elizabethan tradition. Consequently the royalist allusions, though
"fleshless" and conventional for reasons which I have discussed, are not inconsistent with the tone and the purpose of
the early work.

In *Paradise Lost* the use of the "complimentary reference"
presents a more disturbing problem. In the 1620's the Lady
of *Arcades* might quite naturally be called a "rural Queen."
Milton intended no reference to Henrietta, but if such a reference seemed implied it was no cause for worry.

It is another matter to write passage after passage denounc-
ing the courts and palaces and titles of earthly kings, attack-
ing the literary traditions associated with royalism, and then
to employ the royalist allusion as a compliment. Eve is
"majestic," [85]

[85] VIII, 42.

for on her as Queen
A pomp of winning Graces waited still.[86]

It is thus she appears before Raphael—the same Raphael *who scorns to wear the "tedious pomp of Princes."* Are we to assume that the slight to regal appearance given in the description of Raphael is meant to have contemporary reference, but that the queenliness of Eve is to be associated with the royalism of Heaven? If so, we are required to perform imaginative gymnastics! The sure social reference of the royalist idiom has been lost. Its use, even in the conventional allusion, involves contradiction. The poetic royalism of the political anti-royalist is a tortuous thing.

Paradise Lost is a poem of defeat and vicarious revenge. In it the use of a symbolism "trailing clouds of glory" from a broken past is at once inevitable and inappropriate. Milton is forced to affirm what he denies and to deny what he affirms. And, as I have been at some pains to show, he is conscious of his predicament. He struggles for consistency, and fails. He does achieve an unrivalled sweep of fury and power. The anger of Moses and the pageantry of Spenser surge through his lines. Passion and grandeur are here—but confusion, too. Critics and scholars have been compelled to study the thought of the poem apart from the imagery in order to arrive at an understanding of the purpose. But the clash of meaning with the means of expression is not the fault of Milton. It is symptomatic of the age.

In the last two poems Milton seeks to purify his idiom, to control the connotation of the royalist symbol—with what success I shall discuss in the following chapter.

[86] VIII, 60–62.

IV

The Last Poems

§ 1

PARADISE REGAINED and *Samson Agonistes* appeared together in 1671. In discussing the relation of these poems to *Paradise Lost,* Tillyard says: "It is possible that the weakness inherent in the myth of the Fall as a subject compelled him [Milton] to write his last two poems: the first a clear-cut struggle between opposing forces, with good victorious; the second a drama exhibiting the rebirth of heroic energy." [1] For Tillyard the weakness of *Paradise Lost* is due to the fact that "Adam and Eve have no power of heroic virtue. . . . The most powerful expression of heroic energy is found elsewhere." [2] If my interpretation of *Paradise Lost* is correct, it was inevitable that heroic virtue be found "elsewhere," in Heaven, in Hell, in the courts of earthly tyrants—never in Eden. The punitive God had to be justified, his power extolled. In the real world only the few seem just, the many are damned, and deserve to be damned. Such a situation exists. Therefore it must be God's will, even though one had mistakenly hoped for a better than possible world. And may the vengeance of Almighty God smite the ignorant rabble who had betrayed that hope! The weakness of this theme, as far as the complete poetic expression of it is concerned, is in the confusion of values attendant upon the necessary choice of a royalist-power symbolism. I agree with Tillyard that Milton probably felt

[1] Tillyard, pp. 290–291.
[2] P. 290.

compelled to write his last two poems. But not because of a weakness "inherent in the myth of the Fall." The evidence of the text seems to suggest that he is attempting in *Paradise Regained* and *Samson Agonistes* to express separately two of his basic motifs without involving them in the royalist contradiction: the first, the triumph of the Elect, of the aristocratic principle; the second, the apotheosis of vengeance and power.

The anti-democratic element of the first epic reappears in *Paradise Regained*. Not only does Satan slyly suggest that it is the Son's duty to rescue his country "from her Heathen servitude"; the humble fishermen pray to the God of Israel to

> Send thy Messiah forth, the time is come;
> Behold the Kings of the Earth how they oppress
> Thy chosen, to what highth thir pow'r unjust
> They have exalted, and behind them cast
> All fear of thee, arise and vindicate
> Thy Glory, free thy people from thir yoke.[3]

But the Saviour of Man has contempt for the people:

> And what the people but a herd confus'd,
> A miscellaneous rabble, who extol
> Things vulgar, & well weigh'd, scarce worth the praise.
> They praise and they admire they know not what;
> And know not whom, but as one leads the other;
> And what delight to be by such extoll'd,
> To live upon thir tongues and be thir talk,
> Of whom to be disprais'd were no small praise?
> His lot who dares be singularly good.
> *Th' intelligent among them and the wise*
> *Are few, and glory scarce of few is rais'd.*[4]

This is the familiar opposition of the single just man and the blind mob. And, as in *Paradise Lost,* the people deserve the earthly tyrants who reign over them:

[3] II, 43–48.
[4] III, 49–56; italics mine.

> That people victor once, now vile and base,
> *Deservedly made vassal,* who once just,
> Frugal, and mild, and temperate, conquer'd well. . . .
> What wise and valiant man would seek to free
> These thus degenerate, by themselves enslav'd,
> Or could of inward slaves make outward free? [5]

There is no point in political revolution. The Son himself will achieve election through

> things adverse,
> By tribulations, injuries, insults,
> Contempts, and scorns, and snares, and violence,
> Suffering, abstaining, quietly expecting
> Without distrust or doubt.[5]

Glory will be won not by political struggle, but by faith, "inner light," the individual ecstasy of suffering. In the famous rejection of humanist culture, in Book IV, the Saviour not only denies the philosophical spirit, the searching mind of the Greeks (once so dear to Milton); he also repudiates their political thinking:

> Thir Orators thou then extoll'st, as those
> The top of Eloquence, Statists indeed,
> The lovers of thir Country, as may seem;
> But herein to our Prophets far beneath,
> As men divinely taught, and better teaching
> The solid rules of Civil Government
> In thir majestic unaffected stile
> Then all the Oratory of *Greece* and *Rome.*
> In them is plainest taught, and easiest learnt,
> What makes a Nation happy, and keeps it so.[7]

When one remembers that the optimistic republicanism of Milton's revolutionary days was nourished on the examples of Greece and Rome, one realizes that the disillusionment of

[5] IV, 132–145; italics mine.
[6] III, 189–193.
[7] IV, 353–362.

Paradise Regained (and of *Paradise Lost*) entails a rejection of the progressive secular element in humanist thought. The science and the philosophy of humanism can secure neither truth nor the good life. Above all the political science of humanism cannot make nations happy, and keep them so. Milton felt that he had been misled into false hope. In *Paradise Regained* he specifically renounces the wellsprings of his earlier political optimism. The many, the nations, are doomed —for all the arts of Greece and Rome.[8]

This is a re-statement of the "Sons of Light" theme in *Paradise Lost*. It is re-stated because its meaning had been obscured by the royalist symbolism. The "Sons of Light," the single just men, had been opposed sharply to knights and kings of earth. But Christ appeared as a king in battle dress. Not only was he indistinguishable in imaginative terms from earthly kings—he unhappily resembled Satan. In *Paradise Regained* the Son resembles not Satan, not the king in armour, but the Puritan Saint:

> his life
> Private, unactive, calm, contemplative,
> Little suspicious to any King.[9]

He regarded himself as a student and a teacher who preferred the method of salvation by the Word to the method of liberation by the Sword:

> When I was yet a child, no childish play
> To me was pleasing, all my mind was set

---

[8] I cannot accept the view that the implications of Satan's speech are merely dramatic and conventional. Satan consistently symbolizes evil in this poem. Satan's "humanism," in so far as it is a guide to political thinking and action, is rejected as bankrupt by Christ (and by Milton). However, Milton's love for the beauty of classical literature remained, as *Samson Agonistes* will testify.

[9] II, 80–82.

Serious to learn and know, and thence to do
What might be publick good; my self I thought
Born to that end, born to promote all truth,
All righteous things: therefore above my years,
The Law of God I read, and found it sweet,
Made it my whole delight, and in it grew
To such perfection, that e're yet my age
Had measur'd twice six years, at our great Feast
I went into the Temple, there to hear
The Teachers of our Law, and to propose
What might improve my knowledge or their own; . . .
             yet this was not all
To which my Spirit aspir'd, victorious deeds
Flam'd in my heart, heroic acts, one while
To rescue *Israel* from the *Roman* yoke,
Then to subdue and quell o're all the earth
Brute violence and proud Tyrannick pow'r,
Till truth were freed, and equity restor'd:
Yet held it more humane, more heavenly first
By winning words to conquer willing hearts,
And make perswasion do the work of fear.[10]

Christ is created in Milton's own image. Like Milton he spurns pleasure for study. Like Milton he is tempted to change the world by force of arms, by *realpolitik*. Like Milton he turns to the "inner light," to the salvation of "willing hearts," renouncing the secular illusion, ignoring even the plea of innocent men for deliverance from physical tyranny. His mission will be spiritual. Like Milton he will seek "fit audience though few."

When Milton announces in Book I that the poem will "tell of deeds above Heroic" [11] he means what he says. There will be in *Paradise Regained* no vacillation between the praise and blame of the chivalric tradition, no blurring of moral distinctions by the royalist symbol. In *Paradise Lost* Milton's

[10] I, 201–223.
[11] Lines 14–15.

attack on "Heroick Vertu" is cancelled out by Christ the Warrior. In the second epic he puts the denunciation of "Heroick Vertu" into the mouth of Christ himself:

> They err who count it glorious to subdue
> By Conquest far and wide, to over-run
> Large Countries, and in field great Battels win,
> Great Cities by assault: what do these Worthies,
> But rob and spoil, burn, slaughter, and enslave
> Peaceable Nations, neighbouring, or remote,
> Made Captive, . . .
> Then swell with pride, and must be titl'd Gods,
> Great Benefactors of mankind, Deliverers,
> Worship't with Temple, Priest and Sacrifice;
> One is the Son of *Jove,* of *Mars* the other,
> Till Conquerour Death discover them scarce men,
> Rowling in brutish vices, and deform'd,
> Violent or shameful death thir due reward.
> But if there be in glory aught of good,
> *It may by means far different be attain'd*
> *Without ambition, war, or violence;*
> *By deeds of peace, by wisdom eminent,*
> *By patience, temperance.*[12]

As in the parallel passages in *Paradise Lost,* the Arthurian symbol is split, the ornamental military values separated from and opposed to the inner virtues of wisdom and temperance. But in *Paradise Regained* Milton strives to keep this separation, this opposition, consistent. Throughout the poem the power and glory of kings is associated with evil. Wealth and pomp, which in *Paradise Lost* made glorious the courts of God, Satan, and the Kings of earth alike, is in the second epic the bait of Satan, scorned by Christ as vain ornament:

> Witness those antient Empires of the Earth,
> In highth of all thir flowing wealth dissolv'd.[13]

[12] III, 71–92; italics mine.
[13] II, 434–435.

Monarchy, too, is merely Satan's bait. And Christ is not tempted by royal power:

> Thou neither dost perswade me to seek wealth
> For Empires sake, nor Empire to affect
> For glories sake by all thy argument.[14]

When Satan displays the might of earthly kingdoms, Christ replies:

> Much ostentation vain of fleshly arm,
> And fragile arms, much instrument of war
> Long in preparing, soon to nothing brought,
> Before mine eyes thou hast set; and in my ear
> Vented much policy, and projects deep
> Of enemies, of aids, battels and leagues,
> Plausible to the world, to me worth naught.[15]

Note here that the armoury of kings is not only "worth naught"—it is "fragile." Power "plausible to the world" must not be confused with spiritual power. This "luggage of war" [16] is "the argument of human weakness rather then of strength." [17] In other words, Milton carefully dissociates Christ from the royalist symbolism of power which had characterized him in *Paradise Lost*. The strength of God, of Christ, is like the strength of "the single just man." It is spiritual, moral, not to be confused for a moment with the "ostentation vain of fleshly arm." The symbol of power is taken out of Heaven and returned to the corrupt kings of earth.

Satan finally gives up the royalist bait as useless:

> Therefore let pass, as they are transitory,
> The Kingdoms of this world; I shall no more
> Advise thee, gain them as thou canst, or not.

[14] III, 44–47.
[15] III, 387–393.
[16] III, 410..
[17] III, 401–402.

And thou thyself seem'st otherwise inclin'd
Then to a worldly Crown, addicted more
To contemplation and profound dispute.[18]

"The Kingdoms of this world" by Satan's own admission are "transitory." They are "worth naught." They are clearly and consistently associated with evil. In the words of Christ to Satan,

> The Kingdoms of the world to thee were giv'n,
> Permitted rather, and by thee usurp't.[19]

Earthly royalism is Satanic. It is God's gift to Satan, God's vengeance on the unregenerate. God stands apart from the instrument of his vengeance. He *permits* kingship, but he is not imaginatively identified with it as he was in *Paradise Lost*.

So much is obvious. In the main, Milton has rescued God and the Son from contemporary royalist reference. Moral distinctions blurred in *Paradise Lost* are restored. When Satan appears as one "in City or Court, or Palace bred" [20] we know him at once for a villain, a pompous wastrel. We do not admire him. We know perfectly well that we are not meant to admire him. Our points of reference are established. Pomp is vain, evil. Simple, unadorned virtue is good.

However, certain difficulties of expression remain. For instance, Christ's comment on kingship at the end of Book II is puzzling:

> A Crown
> Golden in shew, is but a wreath of thorns,
> Brings dangers, troubles, cares, and sleepless nights
> To him who wears the Regal Diadem,
> When on his shoulders each mans burden lies;

[18] IV, 209–214.
[19] IV, 182–183.
[20] II, 299–300.

> For therein stands the office of a King,
> His Honour, Vertue, Merit and chief Praise,
> That for the Publick all this weight he bears.
> Yet he who reigns within himself, and rules
> Passions, Desires, and Feares, is more a King;
> Which every wise and vertuous man attains:
> And who attains not, ill aspires to rule
> Cities of men, or head-strong Multitudes,
> Subject himself to Anarchy within,
> Or lawless passions in him which he serves.
> But to guide Nations in the way of truth
> By saving Doctrine, and from errour lead
> To know, and knowing worship God aright,
> Is yet more Kingly, this attracts the Soul.[21]

The debt to Shakespeare is apparent. This is the only passage in Milton's poetry where the "inner" values of the royalist symbol are suggested. Here is the Elizabethan conception of the monarch whose "Honour, Vertue, Merit and chief Praise" is his sacrifice of self, his assumption of almost godlike responsibility, his restless concern for each man in his kingdom. True, the proper worship of God is "yet more Kingly," but this implies a positive value in kingship. And if the godless, willful king cannot rule the "headstrong Multitudes" surely the ideal king is more precious by comparison.

The conception of monarchy in this passage seems, at first glance, to contradict the use of royalism in the poem as a whole. Is Milton unaware of this? I think not. The comparison of the crown worn by the ideal king to the "wreath of thorns," the symbol of Christ's martyrdom, is unmistakable in significance. There is the subtle insinuation here that true kingship is possible only for Christ. Mortal kings fall victim to "anarchy within." Dramatically, Milton is making Christ bait Satan. Just as Satan, the opportunist, tempts the hungry

[21] Lines 458–476.

Christ with food, now he tempts him with monarchy. Christ's speech has provided him with an opening. If the speech had been flatly anti-royalist there would have been no more reason to offer thrones than fair women.[22] As it is, Christ has ironically nominated himself as perfect candidate for kingship. Satan loses no time:

> Thy actions to thy words accord, thy words
> To thy large heart give utterance due, thy heart
> Conteins of good, wise, just, the perfect shape.
> Should Kings and Nations from thy mouth consult,
> Thy Counsel would be as the oracle
> *Urim* and *Thummim,* those oraculous gems
> Of *Aaron's* breast: or tongue of Seers old
> Infallible.[23]

The vigor of Christ's refusal to accept an earthly throne quickly dispels any confusion which may have been caused by the dramatic use of an "ideal" royalism. Milton is certainly conscious of the Elizabethan conception of kingship. But that conception is reduced here to a literary device which prompts a wholesale rejection of earthly kingship. Fortunately for the consistency of the poem, the passage is confined to a few lines in a context unmistakably anti-royalist. Nevertheless, one feels that Milton is skating on dangerously thin ice.

There is a much more serious difficulty inherent in the Christ story itself. Christ is rightfully heir to David's throne. In *Paradise Lost* we are told that he has been cheated of his worldly inheritance. Because of the confused and contradictory reference of the royalist symbol in *Paradise Lost* we are not sure but that the physical crown of David is desirable, appropriate for the chivalric warrior of Heaven.

[22] Belial had advised: "Set women in his eye and in his walk" (II, 150). Satan rejects this counsel as futile (II, 172–233).

[23] III, 9–16.

In *Paradise Regained* Milton is careful to dissipate the
earthly connotations of Christ's royalty. He is at pains to show
that the biblical image has no reference to kingship as understood by men. The simple people expect Christ to be their
political deliverer, to ascend his throne. Satan urges him to
take the throne which is rightfully his, which has been
promised him:

> But to a Kingdom thou art born, ordain'd
> To sit upon thy Father *David's* Throne. . . .
> If Kingdom move thee not, let move thee Zeal,
> And Duty; Zeal and Duty are not slow;
> But on Occasions forelock watchful wait.
> They themselves rather are occasion best,
> Zeal of thy Fathers house, Duty to free
> Thy country from her Heathen Servitude;
> So shalt thou best fulfil, best verifie
> The Prophets old, who sung thy endless raign.[24]

Here Milton squarely meets the difficulty of the Bible story.
David's crown is rejected with the others. Milton does not
deny that Christ will inherit a "kingdom." He simply drains
the biblical image of earthly reference. Any notion that the
throne of David promised by Scripture is crudely like the
throne of Caesar (or Charles) is a Satanic illusion. For Christ
consistently scorns the pomp of courts. He appears not as a
warrior, but as a "glorious eremite," [25] "Our Morning Star,
then in his rise." [26] At his baptism the *Spirit* of God descended on him "like a Dove." [27] The angels praise him as

> True Image of the Father, whether *thron'd*
> *In the bosom of bliss, and light of light*
> *Conceiving,* or remote from Heaven, enshrin'd

[24] III, 151–178.
[25] I, 8.
[26] I, 294.
[27] I, 282.

In fleshly Tabernacle, and human form,
Wandring the Wilderness, whatever place,
Habit, or state, or motion, still expressing
The Son of God, *with Godlike force indu'd*.[28]

Significantly, the "godlike force" displayed by the Son on earth is never force of arms.[29] His weapons are temperance, patience, and wisdom—abstract virtues. Significantly, Heaven is described as "light." There Christ is *"enthron'd"* in bliss." As I have said, Milton does not discard the royalist imagery of the Bible. God is "King of Kings." Christ's "raign" will be eternal. But, as in the early poems, God's "kingship" conveys nothing more than rank. It is associated not with the attributes of earthly monarchy (these are clearly denied), but with moral and spiritual qualities. Without doubt Milton has overcome the main confusion of *Paradise Lost*. He has been able to do so by setting aside the power motif of the first epic and concentrating on the single theme of election, of the triumph of the restrictive virtues over evil. It was necessary

[28] IV, 597–603.

[29] The Millenarian ideal of Christ's kingship would seem to have its influence here. While monarchical (and aristocratic in the Puritan sense), Millenarian thought is hostile to all existing kingship. In other words, as in Milton, the symbol of kingship is retained for Christ but the concept is drained of earthly connotation. In this connection it is interesting to note Milton's description of Christ's kingly function in *The Christian Doctrine* (*S.M.*, p. 1009): "The Kingly function of Christ is that whereby being made King by God the Father, he governs and preserves, chiefly by an inward law and spiritual power. . . . Herein it is that the pre-eminent excellency of Christ's kingdom over all others, as well as the divine principles on which it is founded, are manifested; inasmuch as he governs not the bodies of men alone, as the civil magistrate, but their minds and consciences, *and that not by force and fleshly weapons, but by what the world esteems the weakest of all instruments*. Hence external force ought never to be employed in the administration of the kingdom of Christ, which is the church." [Italics mine.] This is surely Millenarian, and in its insistence on "spiritual power" as opposed to "fleshly weapons" it is close to both *Paradise Regained* and *Samson Agonistes* though not to *Paradise Lost*.

to retain the David mythology of the New Testament story. But with the power concept eliminated, *with God's vengeance performed by Satan's kings,* God's title could be emptied of content. Only one passage in *Paradise Regained* suggests that final destruction of the earth which had been a dominant idea in the first epic:

> Know therefore when my season comes to sit
> On *David's* Throne, it shall be like a tree
> Spreading and over-shadowing all the Earth,
> Or as a stone that shall to pieces dash
> All Monarchies besides throughout the world.[30]

A stone will do the deed. Milton is careful never to put a sword in Christ's hand! And the throne is not a throne—but like a tree, with its spreading shadow blotting out the glitter and pomp of the world. Even this brief hint of Christ's power is protected from association with attributes of earthly royalty. "Thou hast conquered, O pale Galilean!" But one feels that the conquest itself has been pale. Clarity has been achieved. Correct moral distinctions have been made. With almost mathematical precision the King of Heaven is distinguished from the earthly king, as the King of Hell is identified with him. The triumph of inner virtue over "fleshly ostentation" is consistent. Yet it is small wonder that critics and readers have always preferred *Paradise Lost,* confused though it be, to *Paradise Regained.* The second epic is negative and dim, except in those passages of temptation where Milton can write sensuous poetry describing evil. The result is that we do not confuse Heaven with Rome, but we find Rome more attractive than Heaven. We are perfectly aware that earthly royalism is Satanic, but it is still exciting. It is more attractive than God's chaste empty title, or the abstrac-

[30] IV, 146–150.

tions which characterize the single just man and Christ. Evil gets concrete expression. Triumphant virtue is negative, unimaginative.

§ 2

In *Samson Agonistes* Milton restates the theme of power and vengeance.[31] This time the agent of revenge is a human figure, a man who had been elected to deliver his people "from Philistine yoke," but who has failed, not through weakness of the body, but through vanity of the spirit. He is restored to strength, and the opportunity for revenge is given him, when he has fully learned the lesson of humility.

Here Milton has set himself the task of giving positive poetic value to those virtues which are presented negatively though triumphantly in *Paradise Regained*. It has been easy enough to condemn "Heroick Vertu." There is still the task of making virtue heroic. Milton had attempted just this in

[31] Revenge in *Samson* is not cosmic. The Mosaic rage of *Paradise Lost* has exhausted itself—"all passion spent." The Philistine captains, lords, and priests are destroyed in the temple. *They are not permitted to live and rule as tyrants over the unregenerate.* There is even hope that the people may profit by Samson's example, since he

> To Israel
> Honour hath left, and freedom, let but them
> Find courage to lay hold on this occasion. [Ll. 1714–1716.]

The clarification of symbolism in the last poems proceeds from a clarification of thought. The careful and conscious art of these poems has demanded rigorous intellectual control. In the process the disappointed rage of *Paradise Lost* is superseded by the humility of *Samson*. There is even a hint of hope —perhaps for a new Arthur. In 1674 Milton was to acclaim Sobieski, the "just man," the *People's elected king*. Milton, of course, was careful to distinguish his new and last kingly hero from kings hitherto known to God and man. Paradoxically, society still had no symbol of leadership to offer the poet other than the crown. One wonders what final tangle Milton would have involved himself in if he had lived to celebrate in poetry this king who was not a king, this symbol not to be confused with the symbol of the same name.

Paradise Lost with confusing results. To avoid the contradic-
tions of that poem it will be necessary, as in *Paradise Regained,* to strip God of royalist symbolism, and to present
the human agent through whom the power of God will work,
as innocent of royalist suggestions. In other words, a new
symbolism was needed in which power and virtue might
merge, as they once did for the Elizabethan in the image of
the Crown. The Crown had been given to Satan. A new idiom
must be found to represent the power of God, the power of
the Saint, if that power was not to be degraded by objectionable associations, if "inner" suggestions of worth were to be
preserved. The theme of *Samson Agonistes* is more difficult
to control than the theme of *Paradise Regained. Even the
titular kingship of God must be eliminated in a poem which
once more identifies God with power.* Not once in *Samson* is
God referred to as "King." He is "the Holy One of Israel," [32]
"God of our Fathers," [33] "the living God." [34] He is an idea,
a principle. His power is made manifest in Samson, who, like
the Christ of *Paradise Regained,* scorns the trappings of chivalry:

> Then put on all thy gorgeous arms, thy Helmet
> And Brigandine of brass, thy broad Habergeon,
> Vant-brass and Greves, and Gauntlet, add thy Spear
> A Weavers beam, and seven-times-folded shield,
> I only with an Oak'n staff will meet thee.[35]

Harapha resents this insult to the ornaments of war:

> Thou durst not thus disparage glorious arms,
> Which greatest Heroes have in battel worn,
> Thir ornament and safety, had not spells

[32] Lines 1427–1428.
[33] Line 667.
[34] Line 1140.
[35] Lines 1119–1123.

And black enchantments, some Magicians Art
Arm'd thee or charm'd thee strong, which thou from Heaven
Feigndst at thy birth was giv'n thee in thy hair.[36]

Harapha knew that it was not the oaken staff or the jawbone
of the ass which had made Samson "an army in himself." It
was black magic. Samson replies:

I know no spells, use no forbidden Arts;
My trust is in the living God who gave me
At my Nativity this strength, diffus'd
No less through all my sinews, joints and bones,
Then thine, while I preserv'd these locks unshorn,
The pledge of my unviolated vow.[37]

This strength is supernatural, transcending and annihilating
the strength of kings, given to Samson not by the King of
Kings but by an Idea. It is itself an idea, not a physical reality.

God, when he gave me strength, to show withal
How slight the gift was, hung it in my Hair.[38]

The strength of the body is nothing. Its fragility is suitably
symbolized in the Hair. Moral weakness or incontinence destroys mere sinew, and leaves Samson "eyeless in Gaza." [39]
The ultimate destruction of the "choice nobility and flower" [40]
of the Philistines, of "Lords, Ladies, Captains, Councellors, or
Priests," [41] is accomplished by Samson's moral victory over
himself. He has put pride behind him. He has learned by suffering to be humble. Of his misfortune "Sole Author I, sole
cause." [42] He comes to regard himself not as a great and
proud deliverer, puffed up with a sense of personal might, the

[36] Lines 1130–1135.
[37] Lines 1139–1144.
[38] Lines 58–59.
[39] Line 41.
[40] Line 1654.
[41] Line 1653.
[42] Line 376.

might of Kings, but as a simple penitent instrument of the Lord's:

> the strife
> With me hath end; all the contest is now
> 'Twixt God and *Dagon*.[43]

The power of the Lord is embodied in the "just men" [44] who *"with Heroic magnitude of mind and celestial vigour arm'd"* [45] render useless the arms and ammunition of kings. When by the exercise of patience and self-abnegation Samson justifies his Election, the strength of God returns and destroys the wicked.

Milton leaves no doubt but that the power which ripped down the pillars of the temple is moral power:

> with head a while enclin'd
> And eyes fast fixt he stood, *as one who pray'd,*
> *Or some great matter in his mind revolv'd.*[46]
> With inward eyes illuminated
> His *fierie vertue* rouz'd
> From under ashes into sudden flame.[47]
>   as an Eagle
> His cloudless thunder bolted on thir heads.
> So *vertue* giv'n for lost,
> Deprest, and overthrown, as seem'd,
> Like that self-begott'n bird
> In the Arabian woods embos't,
> That no second knows nor third,
> And lay e're while a Holocaust,
> From out her ashie womb now teem'd
> Revives, reflourishes, then vigorous most
> When most unactive deem'd.[48]

---

[43] Lines 460–462.
[44] Line 1269.
[45] Lines 1279–1280; italics mine.
[46] Lines 1636–1638; italics mine.
[47] Lines 1689–1691; italics mine. The word "vertue" in Milton often carries with it the suggestion of "power" but, of course, moral power.
[48] Lines 1695–1701; italics mine.

"The eagle," "the phoenix"—these are the final substitutes for the symbol of royalist power. And even these must be labelled carefully with "vertue" and "prayer." The royalist symbol is now admittedly the property of the Devil, and Milton has nothing left to offer God but solemn Puritan abstractions.

Samson Agonistes is a more successful poem than *Paradise Regained*. For one thing, it is not a "second epic" under the shadow of the first. It achieves dignity as well as consistency of style, and formally is perhaps Milton's most perfect performance. Yet one cannot but feel that Milton's care to represent the strength of Samson as supernatural and moral, the manifestation of virtue rather than of sinew, is self-conscious and restrictive. The confusion of *Paradise Lost* must at all costs be avoided. It is avoided. The cost is the vivid and concrete image. Political revolution has forced Milton finally to restrict the range of poetic suggestion. Like Samson, he is shorn of his power symbol. The Elizabethan royalist tradition is at an end.

The Heroic Drama of the Restoration, with its strutting royalist heroes, is a drama of the court, for the court, by the court. It was conceived and enjoyed in defiance of the nation. It deliberately outrages and mocks the bourgeois moral sense, as in the following speech of Aureng-Zebe's:

> How vain is virtue, which directs our ways
> Through certain danger to uncertain praise!
> Barren and airy name! thee Fortune Flies,
> With thy lean train, the pious and the wise.
> Heav'n takes thee at thy word, without regard,
> And lets thee poorly be thy own reward.
> The world is made for the bold, impious man
> Who stops at nothing, seizes all he can.
> Justice to merit does weak aid afford;
> She trusts her balance, and neglects her sword.

Virtue is nice to take what's not her own,
And, while she long consults, the prize is gone.[49]

The hero of the court drama is very like the Harapha of *Samson Agonistes*. He has a sense of honor, the honor of the battlefield (that "Heroick Vertue" which Milton condemned). But he denies the inner moral sense. Dryden's courtly heroes suggest no more than the notions of power and self-congratulation. The style, though bombastic, is deliberate and artificial. The grandiose emotions of the characters are contrived almost mathematically. Love and honor are so neatly and accommodatingly balanced that the opposition between them is always overcome in the nick of time. The juggling of incident to this end is at best dramatic "jig-saw puzzle." Emotional conflicts are never allowed to complicate the process, for they, too, go the way of Euclid. Remarking on this rational structure of Restoration bombast, C. V. Deane [50] sees the influence of the Cartesian doctrine of "clear and distinct perception." Heroism and love are problems in mechanics. Emotions must be dragged into clear couplet consciousness and rhetorically defined.

The drama of kings and mighty warriors has become an artificial exercise in rhetoric. The spontaneity of Marlowe's bombast is gone. The Shakespearian, even the Spenserian, conception of kingship has become unintelligible. It is little wonder that in the intellectual climate of the Restoration Milton should finally deny God the title of King.

[49] Act ii, 500–512.
[50] *Dramatic Theory of the Rhymed Heroic Play, passim.*

V

Conclusion

I SUBMIT that the work of John Milton is of peculiar interest to those critics of our time who regard literature as the expression of civilization rather than as a gift of the gods. Here was a poet who associated himself openly and profoundly with a revolutionary cause, who took his stand on all the important theological, political, and social issues of the day, and who dedicated his poetry to his inmost faith and convictions. The imprint of time and place on his work was inescapable.

My thesis is that *Paradise Lost,* with its rejection of science, of nationalism, of hope for man within the limits of history and society, expresses not only the collapse of the Puritan Revolution, but also marks the end of a great tradition in life and literature—the Elizabethan tradition. This comes out most clearly in the conflict between symbol and idea in *Paradise Lost,* and in Milton's awareness of the conflict. "Concern about symbols is one of the first signs of their disappearance." [1] The disappearance of the royalist symbol in its traditional connotation from *Paradise Regained* and *Samson Agonistes* is not merely a "literary" phenomenon, a detached problem in craftsmanship—it reflects a change in the social order.

The whole question of symbolism in literature is illuminating . . . because *symbols depend directly upon community of belief.* Even the more artificial symbol—such as the symbol derived from

[1] David Daiches, *The Novel and the Modern World,* p. 13.

classical mythology in Renaissance literature—depends, if not
on positive belief of the kind that would motivate action, at least
upon acceptance, upon common knowledge and a common attitude toward that knowledge.[2]

"The community of belief" which guaranteed the royalist
symbol for the Elizabethan artist did not exist for Milton. I
have attempted to show why that was so by placing Milton's
problem against the background of the Elizabethan tradition,
and of the disintegration of that tradition under the stress of
social and economic forces.

The roots of Milton's poetic confusion go deep. His aristocratic idealism, derived as much from Plato as from Calvin
and given flesh by Spenser, was never at home in the Puritan
Revolution. Milton never understood the socio-economic implications of the "good old cause." True, he came to see that
"new Presbyter was but old priest writ large," and that Cromwell was something less than God's right arm. He even attacked the London bankers for selfish materialism. But it
never occurred to him that the acquisitive spirit was the fundamental dynamic of the revolution; that there was never a
"Restoration" in the full sense of the word; and that the
"middle-sort of men" had won after all.

Passionately dedicated to the ends he has conceived, he is concerned solely with the quickest way of achieving them. If men refuse to be free, they must be dragooned into righteousness and
liberty. Milton was therefore able to transfer his support—as he so
frequently did—to any group or individual who seemed capable
of imposing that order. Disillusion is the central theme of his experience. And the failure of every group in whom he rested his
hope for the realization of his ideal made him increasingly bitter
and impatient.[3]

[2] *The Novel and the Modern World*, p. 13; italics mine.
[3] David W. Petegorsky, "Milton as Social Philosopher," *The New Republic*, Vol. 104, no. 17, p. 606.

"The ends he has conceived" were not the ends of the Puritan Revolution. His ideals—religious, philosophical, literary—could no more be imposed on the politics of the age than the royal crown could be placed on the head of "a single just man." He came to believe that political humanism had failed him—that science, and nationalism, and social progress were illusions. His eclectic culture, with its Elizabethan and classical elements, had played him false. Fallen man could not inherit the earth. And so Milton finally took comfort in ethical and theological abstractions, in a static world of values where the fleshless aristocratic ideal might persist unchanging and unchangeable.

At the height of Elizabethan culture the aspirations of the individual soul could be identified imaginatively with the aspirations of the nation. Qualities of worth and spiritual excellence could be and were suggested by the use of the royalist symbol. The vision of the ideal emerged out of the stuff of reality itself. There was a "community of belief." In Milton's work there is evident not only the breakdown of this community" (as his self-conscious concern with symbolism shows), but also a sharpening contradiction between the individual and society, between moral values and social realities, between ends and means. Milton's ideology, based on metaphysical speculation and his knowledge of past example, could neither interpret nor direct the phenomenon of capitalist economy which had brought to an end the "Elizabethan compromise," and which had finally plunged England into civil war. In the chaos Milton searched for his lost, crownless Arthur.

Milton's predicament was fundamentally the predicament of the artist in a period of revolutionary crisis. His work is important for us, among other reasons, because it illustrates the problem of literature in a changing society, a problem which the creative artist of our own day must solve, or attempt to solve. The sociological problem is once more engaging our attention. During the last decade the battle of "left" and "right" engrossed us as completely as the battle of "ancients and moderns" once engrossed our rather remote ancestors. For every literary escape into the "Cult of Unintelligibility" we had an excursion by play, poem, or novel into the utterly intelligible idiom of the factory or union hall. For every "reactionary essay" we had a proletarian manifesto. New aesthetic problems are being erupted again. The crater was not extinct. Even the classical calm of Mr. Eliot's criticism could not hide the agitation of his poetry and the poetry of his generation.

To-day traditional ideals and the literary techniques proper to their expression are being attacked by the sociological critic and abandoned by the socially-minded writer. Critics like Daiches, Burgum, and Cowley point to a growing social consciousness in our literature, and to an increasing reliance on "public speech," on language charged with popular idiom and with symbols which depend for their validity on social and political reference. The new poets are trying to slough off the coils of Mr. Eliot's *Waste Land* technique which had entwined our literary expression for a decade and which had begun to strangle it. In thought and in manner *The Waste Land* represented a prostrate culture strewn with the fragments of the past, arid, incapable of new impressions. It may be significant that *Paradise Lost* was written *after* the battle, *after* the failure of a revolution which had seemed to promise a golden Utopia. The *Waste Land* School was dedicated to defeat before the battle. It expressed the weariness, the sickness of a culture which bears aloft no new banners. Eliot and his followers were convinced of the truth of T. E. Hulme's dictum that the twentieth century had inherited "the sloppy dregs of the Renaissance."

This dictum, this assumption of decay and defeat, has been rigorously denied not only by the Marxians but also by "left" democrats like Archibald MacLeish and Meyer Levin. A new "community of belief" is being forged in the resurgence of the democratic faith, a faith both collectivist and individualist, both economic and political. From Day Lewis to J. B. Priestley writers are turning to the common experiences of the common man for themes and for symbols.

The difficulties in the way of such a literary Renaissance need not be minimized. As in Milton's day, the artist concerned with the social problem is buffeted and often sent sprawling by the winds of doctrine which blow from the storm centres. We have our "Levellers," our "True Levellers," our "Ranters," and our "middle sort." The "community of belief" for artist and audience is not easily attained in a welter of ideological confusion.

Even for the Marxians who challenge the future armed with a clear-cut world-view and who therefore write with clearly defined symbols, the problem of communication is by no means an easy one. A poet like C. Day Lewis has not only the task of coining a revolutionary symbolism, he has also the task of impressing it on a generation of readers trained in the associative gambits of the nineteenth century. True, details of working-class experience can be woven into new patterns of evocations. The strike, the picket-line, the barricade suggest new symbols of power to the "left" poet, symbols compatible with Marxian ideology. He is not forced to make his hero a banker as Milton was forced to make his God a king! Society has provided him with new images. But whereas

Milton had to make use of symbols which belonged to the past, the radical poet of the twentieth century makes use of symbols which belong to the future, or rather which depend for full understanding by a wide audience on the democratic advance of the working class. Hence the apparent obscurity of much of our radical poetry:

A radical poet who chose to speak of the red woman (meaning revolution) was likely to be misunderstood as referring to a scarlet woman. When the same poet tried to express the idea that revolution would destroy capitalism and ended his poem smashingly with an image of the red woman's teeth as a guillotine, such an image was, to say the least, absurd. The trouble, in other words, which the revolutionary poets met in attempting to express their social philosophy was partly one of technique in the use of language and partly one of subject matter. The obscurity in revolutionary poetry is due, in fact, at least in part, to the poet's having identified himself fairly exclusively with a small section of society—with the more radical thinkers. He is in a sense a step ahead of his time, for he speaks for labor when labor remains more or less inarticulate, and for successful revolution when such revolution is wishful thinking on the part of the poet. Moreover, though he thinks himself the voice of the working-class, the poet is read, if at all by the middle-classes. . . . He runs the danger of arousing, by the special class-conscious terminology he employs, the wrong responses. The way out of this predicament is not clear.[4]

The example of revolutionary imagery in this quotation is perhaps not well-chosen, but the passage serves to illustrate the point that the "left" poet of our generation has not as yet the wide essential "community of belief" to support his symbolism. By its very nature our radical poetry is a poetry of struggle reflecting class division. It is the poetry of transition.

Many of our "revolutionary" writers are essentially middle-class in training and background. They are not at home with

[4] *This Generation*, ed. George K. Anderson and Eda Lou Walton, p. 581.

new symbols which they have abstracted from second-hand accounts of working-class experience. Spender, Auden,[5] and Lewis are from the aristocracy. One suspects that Spender in particular "seeks to escape pessimism by discovering the old aristocratic virtues in the lower classes, and especially in their leaders."[6] And the old language, the old imagery is not easily dismissed from the poetic blood-stream of the new recruits to the working class. As Edwin Berry Bergum shrewdly notes of a passage from Spender:

The following lines are certainly, for all their brave sound, inadequate as an account of the way in which a revolution should appeal to a revolutionary poet:

Through torn-down portions of old fabric let their eyes
Watch the admiring dawn explode like a shell
Around us, dazing us with its light like snow.

The passive position of watching the dawn is hardly fitting to the revolutionary; nor should the dawn daze like snow those who under self-discipline have known what to expect and are ready for the next move. A revolution is not to be described in terms appropriate to Dante's mystic union with God.[7]

The "left" poet, then, has not only to make his new symbols intelligible, he has to discard the descriptive imagistic habits of the past when those habits contradict his meaning and in-

[5] It is interesting to note that W. H. Auden, alienated not only from Marxism but from hope in successful collective democratic action, has abandoned popular social symbolism. In his recent volume, *The Double Man,* he makes symbols of the "priests, prophets, and healers who were admired in the Reich before Hitler" (Malcolm Cowley, "Auden in America," *New Republic,* April 7, 1941). Since his political disillusionment Auden has retreated towards the "Cult of Unintelligibility," and towards metaphysical abstraction. Cowley draws a parallel with the revulsion of the English romantics against the French Revolution.

[6] Edwin Berry Burgum, "Three Radical Poets," *Proletarian Literature in the United States,* p. 331.

[7] "Three Radical Poets," p. 333.

tention. This, of course, was precisely Milton's problem. Fortunately for the contemporary artist the new set of symbols
has emerged. And despite the difficulties of expression which
I have described, the left-wing poet is learning to make effective and evocative use of his symbolism. This is particularly true of men who write from active personal experience
in the working-class movement. I shall quote a short poem by
just such a writer, Edwin Rolfe:

DEFINITION

Knowing this man who calls himself comrade,
mean, underhand, lacking all attributes
real men desire, that replenish all worlds
men strive for; knowing that charlatan, fool, too,
masquerading always in our colors, must also
be addressed as comrade—knowing these
and others to be false, deficient in knowledge
and love for fellow men that motivates our kind,
nevertheless I answer the salutation proudly
equally sure that no one can defile it,
feeling deeper than the world the love it bears,
the world it builds. And no man, lying,
talking behind back, betraying trustful friend,
is worth enough to soil this word or mar this world.[8]

For Rolfe the word "comrade" has an inner value of knowledge, love, hope, and power. It is a symbol in which the individual merges with the group, with revolutionary faith, with
mankind. For Rolfe the symbol cannot be defiled by false
individual "comrades" any more than for Shakespeare the
royalist symbol could be defiled by a weak king. There is a
reference back to a central experience which is not disturbed
by the exception. In this poetry the conflict between the idea
and the fact, between the individual and society, between
moral values and social realities has been resolved.

[8] Reprinted in *This Generation*, p. 782.

However, the "community of belief" upon which such a resolution depends is necessarily narrow. The widening of the "community of belief" depends on a widening of democracy. It has been my purpose merely to point the analogy between Milton's problem and the problem of the revolutionary writer of the 1930's. The war has created fresh difficulties for the contemporary artist too intricate for analysis here.[9] However, the generalization stands. For Rolfe, for Day Lewis, for Fearing—as for John Milton—*the validity of symbols with social reference* is determined by society, and not by the genius of the individual, however great that genius be. The artist, if the moment is ripe for him, may help to change his world. But he is himself changed in the process. He is a social animal.

[9] For a clear discussion of the impact of the present war on art, see Edwin Berry Burgum, "Art in Wartime," *Science and Society*, Vol. VI, no. 4, pp. 331–351.

Index

149